The Vestry Book of South Farnham Parish Essex County, Virginia 1739-1779

Ann K. Blomquist

HERITAGE BOOKS
2006

HERITAGE BOOKS
AN IMPRINT OF HERITAGE BOOKS, INC.

Books, CDs, and more—Worldwide

For our listing of thousands of titles see our website
at
www.HeritageBooks.com

Published 2006 by
HERITAGE BOOKS, INC.
Publishing Division
65 East Main Street
Westminster, Maryland 21157-5026

Copyright © 2005 Ann K. Blomquist

Other books by the author:
Goochland County, Virginia Court Order Book 3, 1731-1735
*Southam Parish Land Processioning, 1747-1784
Goochland, Cumberland, and Powhatan Counties, Virginia*
The Vestry Book of Southam Parish, Cumberland County, Virginia, 1745-1792

All rights reserved. No part of this book may be reproduced or transmitted in any form or by any means, electronic or mechanical, including photocopying, recording or by any information storage and retrieval system without written permission from the author, except for the inclusion of brief quotations in a review.

International Standard Book Number: 978-0-7884-3191-9

Contents

Introduction
History of the Parish i
Parish Officials iii
Parish Properties iv
Ministers iv
Vestry Records v
Editorial Notes and Methods vii

Sample Pages x

Parish Map xii

The Vestry Book 1

Appendices
A. Vestry Officials 156
B. Glossary and Abbreviations 159

Bibliography 160

Index 162

INTRODUCTION

The Vestry Book of South Farnham Parish contains the processioning records of the parish for the years 1739-1779. While the processioning orders and returns are recorded in this volume, the parish business meetings were maintained in some separate volume which no longer exists. Though we wish those proceedings were extant, we can be delighted that these fairly complete parish processioning descriptions are available.

History of the Parish

The area along the southern shore of the Rappahannock River experienced many changes before reaching its final colonial form of South Farnham Parish. Charles River, one of the original shires of 1634, included the remote territory that would later be South Farnham Parish in Essex County. The name Charles River was given to the shire and the parish. In 1643, the county name changed to York though the parish retained the Charles River name.[1] As the population increased, new counties were needed. In 1651, land was taken from York for the creation of Lancaster and Northumberland counties. No name was assigned to the parish, but this circumstance was brief. By 1654, the area was the Upper Parish of Lancaster County.[2]

The year 1656 brought two changes. Rappahannock County was formed from the upper region of Lancaster and Farnham Parish was created to coincide with the new county. The pressures of a growing population caused continual changes. Two parishes were needed in the county, so in 1661, Farnham Parish was reduced by the formation of Sittenburne (Sittingbourne) Parish.[3] Farnham Parish then remained stable for over twenty years. But in 1684, the parish was reduced again, being divided into South Farnham (south of the Rappahannock River) and North Farnham.

Rappahannock County was dissolved in 1692 with the creation of Essex County and Richmond County.[4] During this time period, Essex County and South Farnham Parish coincided in their boundaries. In 1704, the northwestern section of the parish was taken to form St. Anne's

Parish.⁵ With this last major change, South Farnham Parish assumed the shape that it retained until its demise after the American Revolution. Two parishes existed in Essex County with South Farnham Parish comprising the southern two-thirds of the county.

The following chart summarizes the changes:

Year	Parish	County
1634	Charles River Parish	Charles River County
1643	Charles River Parish	York County
1651	Unnamed Parish	Lancaster County
1654	Upper Parish	Lancaster County
1656	Farnham Parish	Rappahannock County
1661	Farnham Parish reduced	Rappahannock County
1684	South Farnham Parish	Rappahannock County
1692	South Farnham Parish	Essex County
1704	South Farnham reduced	Essex County

Though all residents of Virginia were required to attend and support the Established Church, dissident citizens were tolerated. In 1758, the following men notified the Court that they intended to establish a Presbyterian Church on the land of Thomas Miller: William Amis, Francis Brown, John Bush, John Clark, Robert Clark, Thomas Clark, Thomas Cox, Richard Crittenden, Josiah Daly, John Davis, Thomas Denet, Benjamin Dunn, James Dunn, Nathaniel Dunn, Thomas Dunn, William Dunn Jr, Titus Ferguson, William Gording, Thomas Johnson, John Jones, Phillip Kidd, Josiah Mactyer, James Medley Sr, Abraham Montague, William Parr, William Ramsey, William Ramsey Jr, John Roden, George Russell, John Sadler, Alexander Smith, Benjamin Smith, John Smith, Richard St. John, Henry Street, Arthur Tate, James Turner, John Wily, Isaac Williams, John Williamson, Leonard Williamson.⁶

Quakers, Presbyterians, Methodists, and Baptists quietly grew throughout Virginia beginning in the 1740s. Then the rapid rise of dissident Protestant sects in the 1770s alarmed county officials. Baptists started the Upper Essex Baptist Church in late 1772, but by 1774, the Baptist ministers attempting to form Piscataway Baptist Church were met with stiffer resistance and were arrested.⁷

After the Revolution, county dissidents were active in their insistence on religious freedom and no state-sanctioned support for the Anglican Church. The year 1785 brought the defeat of the assessment bill for the former Established Church by the Virginia Assembly.[8] South Farnham and its sister parishes throughout Virginia ceased to function as governmental institutions and reorganized as the Protestant Episcopal Church.

For the years covered by this vestry book, South Farnham Parish was bounded as follows: on the northeast by the Rappahannock River, on the southeast by Middlesex County, on the southwest by King and Queen County, and on the northwest by St. Anne's Parish of Essex County. South Farnham encompassed about 175 square miles while the whole of Essex County includes about 261. In 1770, a small piece at the north end of South Farnham Parish was transferred to St. Anne's Parish.[9]

Parish Officials

During the colonial era, a parish required the services of a variety of people. Paid positions included the minister, clerk of the vestry, clerks (readers) of the churches, sextons, and the tithe collector. The vestrymen, church wardens, and processioners received no compensation.

The law directed that twelve responsible men who subscribed to the beliefs and discipline of the Church of England be selected as vestrymen. Their duties included promoting religious life, keeping the parish accounts, ordering the care of the poor and needy, employing the minister, keeping parish records, maintaining the parish property, and tending to all other parish business.

There were usually two churchwardens who acted as the executive officers of the vestry, being responsible for implementing the orders of the vestrymen. The clerk of the vestry recorded the parish business in the vestry books. Because this volume contains only the processioning records, there would have been other books which contained the parish accounts and the parish register of births, marriages, and deaths. John Vass held the position of Clerk of the Vestry for at least 1739 through his death in 1755 when his son Henry Vass was appointed.

This vestry book provides the names of only the ministers, vestrymen, and clerks of the vestry. The records of the business meetings would identify many other people who were contributing to the work of the parish in the community.

Appendix A includes a list of the officials known from this record.

Parish Properties

Normally, a colonial parish would own and maintain several churches and a glebe as the residence of the parish minister. If the vestry business meetings of this parish were extant for this time period, there would be orders concerning the properties. None of the parish properties were mentioned in this record book. Glebe Creek is the only hint of that parish entity.

More detailed information about the properties can be found in E. Lee Shephard's *A History of St. Paul's Episcopal Church*, Bishop Mead's *Old Churches, Ministers, and Families of Virginia*, and James Slaughter's *Settlers, Southerners, Americans: The History of Essex County, Virginia 1608-1984*.[10]

Ministers

The ministers who served South Farnham Parish during the period of this record book were Rev. William Phillips, Rev. William Stuart, and Rev. Alexander Cruden.

For a few years prior to this record, the ministry of South Farnham had been vacant. Rev. Henry Shorthose served the parish for 1735-1736, but after his death in 1736, the post went unfilled until about 1739.[11] By the summer of 1739, William Phillips was serving as the rector. Born about 1708 in England, Phillips had been educated at Merton College, Oxford. He worked as a private tutor in Virginia for 1731-1734, but returned to England to be ordained.[12] His name appears at the July 1739 vestry meeting. He remained in South Farnham about five years until the end of 1744.

The next minister appears only briefly in the record book. Rev. William Stuart (1723-1798) had been licensed to preach in September 1746 and received his King's Bounty in October 1746.[13] His father Rev. David Stuart was the parish minister of St. Paul's Parish in King George County. Rev. Stuart attended the vestry meeting on July 21, 1747, when processioning orders were given for the parish. Though this is the only reference to Stuart in the vestry book, he may have been in the parish for several years. By 1749, he had settled in his father's parish where he succeeded his father.[14]

After a vacancy in the rectorship of several years, Rev. Alexander

Cruden arrived to fill the void. A native of Scotland, he had been ordained in March 1749. By July 1751, Cruden had begun his long tenure with the parish. While the next 25 years may have been pleasant and peaceful, the end of his term reflected the tumult of the coming Revolution. Like many of his Anglican colleagues, Cruden supported the King's cause. When he refused to take an oath of support to the Commonwealth of Virginia in the summer of 1776, the parish removed him.[15] After lingering in Virginia until early 1778, Cruden retreated to England.[16]

During the upheaval of the American Revolution, there was no minister for South Farnham Parish.

Appendix A includes a list of the colonial parish ministers.

Vestry Records

The Clerks of the Vestry used this book to record only the processioning records of the parish. The results of the business meetings and the register of births, marriages, and deaths must have been placed in other volumes which have not survived.[17]

Processioning was an important parish process. For the colonial parishes where both the processioning orders and returns still exist, processioning usually comprises over half of the written records.[18] Every four years, each parish was divided into "so many precincts as to them shall seem most convenient for processioning every particular person's lands."[19] For South Farnham, this convenient number was twenty precincts until 1771 when it was slightly changed to nineteen.

The four year cycle of processioning in South Farnham included the years 1739, 1743, 1747, 1751, 1755, 1759, 1763, 1771, 1775, and 1779. There is no stated reason for the omission of 1767 though that year was also skipped in Southam Parish of Cumberland County.[20]

When the vestry met, the list of attendees was usually recorded in the order of the minister, the churchwardens, the vestrymen. Most vestry meetings did not include the full complement of officials. Sometimes only one churchwarden was present, while the number of vestrymen varied from four to nine. Unfortunately, no vestrymen were listed for 1747, 1751, or 1763.

The assignment of processioners to their precincts was usually made in July or August, though the last three processionings were ordered in

October, with the returns entered the next year.[21] For each precinct, the vestry was supposed to appoint "two intelligent honest freeholders at least to see such processioning performed." For South Farnham, three processioners were usually selected.

Though the law required that the processioners file their returns, the penalty for failure to complete their task was a fine which does not seem to have intimidated any negligent processioners. Processioners were remiss in the actual processioning or the filing of their returns for a variety of reasons: deaths, illnesses, poor weather, moving out of the parish. Thus, the return rates vary considerably. The following chart summarizes the processioning results.

Year	# precincts	# returns	% returns
1739	20	20	100%
1743	20	20	100%
1747	20	0	0%
1751	20	11	55%
1755	20	16	80%
1759	20	12	60%
1763	20	7	35%
1771	19	13	65%
1775	19	0	0%
1779	19	0	0%

The first three sets of precinct returns were randomly recorded, but the final four sets (1775, 1759, 1763, and 1771) were carefully listed in their numerical order, with black space left in anticipation of absent returns.

Though the returns are repetitive and ordinary, a few unusual items appear. There were two men named William Dunn. They were distinguished as "William Dunn (W)" and "William Dunn (B)" and, in 1771, further delineated as "William Dunn (white)" and "William Dunn (black)." Whether these designations refer to race is unknown, but the same listing of "William Dunn (White)" was included in the 1769 list of county voters.[22]

One of the objectives of regular processioning was the reduction of boundary disputes. However, contained in this vestry book is a dispute between William Lowry (Lourie) as the first party and John Robinson and Francis Smith as the second party. A jury was summoned but they deferred to the judgment of Robert Broocke, the surveyor, and the plat (pages 25 and 26).

Though middle names were unusual during this era, a few men were identified with three names: Thomas Henry Broocke, Robert Sp Coleman (Sp for Spilsby), Thomas Cooper Dickerson, Richard Thomas Haile, John Davis Hall, Robert Payne Waring.[23]

Editorial Notes and Methods

The original vestry book for South Farnham Parish, which is usually stored in an bank vault, is in the care of St. John's Episcopal Church of Tappahannock, Virginia. Measuring 7.125" by 18.25", the original is in excellent condition with only a few loose pages. The writing is very legible throughout the book though very small towards the end of the record.

After disestablishment of the Anglican Church, the Episcopal Church in Virginia reorganized and survived. The vestry book continued to be used for vestry minutes (1819-1827, 1833-1876), the parish register (1825-1875), and some miscellaneous records.

This transcription is based on the microfilm of the original book provided by the Library of Virginia. Unfortunately, in the current microfilm copy, the tops and bottoms of many pages are unreadable due to the filming process. In some cases, entire pages are unreadable. A visit to view the original book was required for transcription of those sections of the book. Because of deliberate limited access to the original book, careful proofreading of the unreadable sections could not be accomplished.

The clerk of the vestry started this record on the lefthand page. This places the odd numbered pages on the left and the evens on the right, reverse from the normal page numbering system. On the microfilm copy and in the original book, there are no page numbers, but the pages of the book have since been numbered in pencil, with page number one on the left. Because some of the first pages are loose, they were microfilmed in the wrong order. The microfilm shows pages 1, 4, 5, 2, 3, 6 and then continues in the correct order. For the researcher who wishes to refer to the original book, the page numbers have been denoted in brackets [ ]. The microfilm is available from the Library of Virginia as Miscellaneous Reel 577.

Throughout this book, the handwriting of the vestry clerks is very legible. Style decisions, however, were needed for the printed transcription. My overall philosophy has been to change as little of the original record as possible. Attempting to preserve the flavor of colonial writing, I have retained superscripts, capital letters, and spelling. To aid the reader, the names of individuals and places have been capitalized and some punctuation has been modernized. Flourishes, long dashes, and decorative marks have been omitted. Spelling is, not surprisingly, rather variable.

This vestry book covers the time period when the method of recording dates was changed. Through 1751, the first day of the year was considered to be March 25 with January and February as the last months of the year. So, January and February were written in a different style, for example, January 13, 1750/1 would mean January 13, 1751 to modern readers. Calendar reform finally reached the colonies in September 1752 when 11 days were removed from the calendar and the first day of the year was set at January 1. Prior to September 1752, the vestry meetings dated for the months of January and February may appear to be out of order, but the reader should realize that those meetings actually should be numbered with the next year. Dates after September 1752 are in the modern form.

This project would only be possible with the help of others. The editor wishes to make grateful acknowledgment to the Library of Virginia, to John Blomquist for his computer wizardry, support and encouragements; and to my family for their support and encouragement..

June 2004   Ann Kicker Blomquist
Orlando, Florida

Notes

1. Cocke, 141.
2. Cocke, 142.
3. Mason, 4; Cocke, 144-145.
4. 3 Hening 104.
5. *William and Mary Quarterly* (2) 23, 108.
6. Hopewell, "Presbyterians," 41.
7. Shepard, 27; Slaughter, 75-82.
8. Slaughter, 80.
9. 8 Hening 406; Cocke, 207.
10. Shepard, 13-15; Mead, 389-395; Slaughter, 18-20, 75-80.
11. Shepard, 15-16.
12. Weis, 41; Shepard, 16.
13. Weis, 49; Shepard, 17.
14. Weis, 49; Shepard, 18.
15. Shepard, 26-29.
16. Weis, 12.
17. Shepard, 13; Gaidmore, 79.
18. Some parish books which include processioning records are the Upper Parish of Nansemond County, Southam Parish of Cumberland and Powhatan Counties, St. Paul's Parish of Hanover County.
19. This phrasing was used in every processioning order for South Farnham.
20. Blomquist, xiii.
21. The order dates, beginning in 1739, were July 25, July 11, July 16, August 27, July 29, July 9, August 4, October 8, October 27, and October 1.
22. Hopewell, "Voters," 169.
23. Some of these full names also appear in Dorman's index and Hopewell's "Voters."

19th. Ordered that John Hill Edmund Pagett and William Webb or any two Procession Every Persons Lands in their Precinct Between Col. Waring's Mill and Henry Tandy's and up to Charles Wallace from thence to Mr. James Reynolds Begining the Tenth day of Decr. and to Finish by the last day of January and to make their Return as the Law directs —

20th. Ordered that Leonard Hill William Hopkins and Rich. Hill Junr. or any Two Procession Every persons Lands in the Upper Precinct to King & Queen Begining the Twelfth day of Decr. & to finish by the last day of January and to make their Return as the Law directs —

Signed
John Upshaw } Church Wardens
William Young

Truly Registered pr. Henry Vass Clk of the Vestry

At a vestry held for Southfarnham Parish at Mr. William Daggs Piscataway Ferry on the 5th Day of Octobr. 1764

Present
John Upshaw } Church Wardens
Samuel Beachey

James Webb John Clements Thomas Roane William Mountague William Young and Archibald Ritchie Gentn.

It is Ordered that the Returns made by the Processioners be truly Registered in the Vestry Book appointed for that Purpose and that they be Examd. over by the Vestry to see that they be Rightly Entered within six months after ye date hereof

John Upshaw
Samuel Beachey

Portion of page 81 from the Vestry Book
showing 1763 processioning orders

Wm. Brooke Prevent ____ The Line Between Col. Corbin and M.
John Beale Baler Brooke Prevent ____ The Line Between Col. Corbin
and Mr. Rich. Adm. Baler Brooke Prevent ____ The Line Between Mr.
John Beale and Henry Vass James Medley Senr. Prevent ____ The Line
Between P. Beale and James Medley Senr. P. Medley Senr. Prevent ____
The Line Between Ja. Medley Senr. and Charles Sanders Decd. Orphan P.
Medley Prevent ____ The Line Between John Boughton and Birds Orphan
John Boughton Prevent ____ The Line Between Joshua Boughton and Alex.
S. Sanders John Boughton Senr. Prevent ____ The Line Between Mr. Rich.
Adm. and Mr. John Beales Back Land is not to be found also the Line
Between Adm. and Henry Vass not to be found also the Line Between Henry
Vass and Charles Sanders Decd. Orphan not to be found . . . .

Given under our hands   James Medley Jr
                           Thomas Watts
                           Joshua Boughton

For Obedience to an order of Vestry made on the 4th Day of August 1763
We the Subscribers hath processiond the Lines as Followeth.
Nov. 24. The Line between Mr. Adams and George Bird, processiond. The Line
Between Mr. Adams and George Russell processiond The Line between
Mr. Adams and William Mountague, processiond The Line between
George Bird Gent. and William Mountague processiond The Line
Between Joshua Boughton Wm. Brooke & George Newbill processiond
Nov. 25. The Line between Samuel Brooke and Isaac Williams processiond
The Line between Samuel Brooke and John Brooke processiond
The Line between Samuel Brooke and the heirs of John Philips
Processiond The Line Between Samuel Brooke and the heirs of John
Evans processiond The Line between John Brooke and Henry Gardner
Processiond The Line between Henry Gardner and Samuel Brooke
Processiond The Line between Henry Gardner and Wm. in presence
Evans processiond also another Line between Henry Gar-
above Said Heirs From the main Road up the Lower izindine
Beals old Line through the old Field, processiond peaceindine
                    Turn over

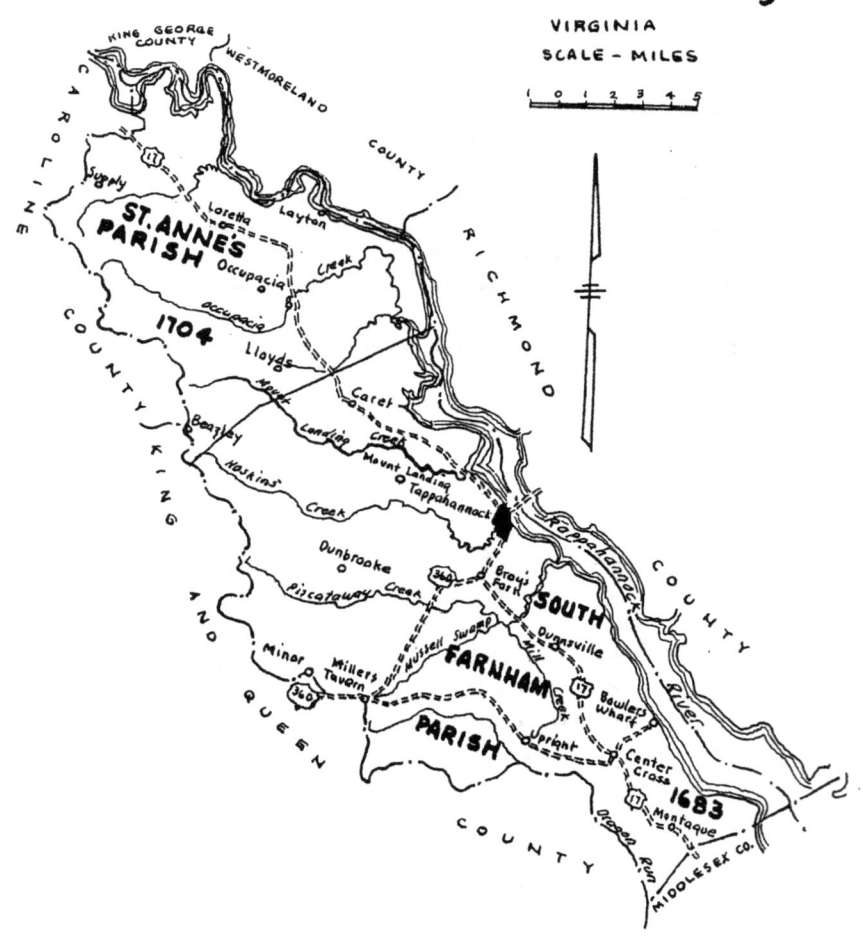

Map from
Charles Cocke
Parish Lines of the Diocese of Southern Virginia

The Vestry Book of South Farnham Parish

[1]   [1739 Processioning]
At a Vestry held for the parrish of South Farnham at Piscataway Ferry the 25th day of July 1739.

Present
The Rever^d William Philips
The Hona^ble John Robinson Esqr Church Warden
Capt Nicholas Smith Capt William Roan M^r: William Covington M^r: Isaac Scandret M^r: Jno: Vass

Pursuant to an order of Court for the County of Essex bareing date of 25th day of July 1739 whereby it is ordered that the Vestry of each parish within the s^d County divide their parishes into so many precincts as to them shall seem most convenient for processioning every particular persons Lands in the severall parishes & appoint the particular times for processioning, likewise appoint two intelligent honest freeholders at least of every precinct to see such processioning performed; & take & return to the Vestry an acc^t of Every persons Land they shall procession and of the persons present at the same and what land in their precincts they shall fail to procession and of the particular reasons of such failure.

This present Vestry do therefore divide the parish of South Farnham into twenty precincts and it is ordered that Rice Jones John Bush & Abraham Mountague or any two of you procession every persons land in your precinct beginning at the lower end of Essex County & run to the Gleab Creek from thence at M^r. Joshua Frys Quarter on the Dragon & make their return as the law directs beginning ye tenth day of Novemb^r & to finish by the last of the same month.

Ordered that Joshua Boughton John Boughton & Jno: Vass or any two of you procession the lands in your precincts: Beginning at Mr Frys Quarter on the Dragon from thence to Joshua Boughtons & so to ye Dragon from thence to Mrs Adams Quarter on the River Side Bowlers Ferry Beginning the fifteenth day of Novemb^r & to finish by the last day of the same month and make their return as the law directs.

Ordered that Nicholas Smith jun^r Thom^s Broocke & Jn° Cheney or any two of you procession the land in your precinct beginning at Joshua Boughtons from thence up to John Dickes from thence to William Cheneys on the Dragon beginning the twentieth day of November & to finish by the twentieth day of December and make their return as the law directs.

Ordered that John Webb Hugh Williams & John Young or any two of you procession every persons land in your precinct beginning at M^rs: Adams land on the River Side from thence to Mr Tylers Creek by John Hays and so to the Back Road by Thom^s Cauthorn from thence down the s^d Road to Joshua Boughtons beginning the twenty second day of November & to finish by the twenty second day of Decemb^r & make their return as the law directs.

Ordered that John Evans Richd Beale & Ludy Piles or any two of them procession every persons land in your precinct Beginning at Coll Robinsons Quarter land by Thom^s: Cauthorn from thence to John Dickes from thence down the Mill Swamp to Piscatua Ferry so down the Main Road to Co^ll Robinsons Quarter old field beginning the twenty sixth day of Novemb^r and to finish by ye twenty second day of Decemb^r & make their return as the Law directs.

[2]   [1739 Processioning]
Ordered that Henry Young James Webb & Piscataway John Webb or any two of you procession every persons land in your precinct Beginning at Col^l Robinsons Qu^r Land by Thom^s: Cauthorns from thence to ye Creek by John Philips and all the land between ye River and the Road to Piscatua Creek beginning the Twenty Eighth day of Novemb^r & to finish by the first day of Jany and make their return as the Law directs.

Ordered that Dan^ll Dobyns Richd Bush & John Hardy or any two of you procession every persons [land] in your precinct Beginning at William

Chaneys on the Dragon from thence to the head of the Covingtons Mill Swamp and down the Swamp to Co[ll] Tayloes Qu[r] landing from thence up the Road by Thom[s]: Williamsons to William Chaneys beginning the third day of Decemb[r] & to finish by the twelfth day of Jan[y] & make their return as the Law directs.

Ordered that James Turner James Boughan & Jn[o] Tyler or any two of them procession Every persons land in their precinct beginning at Col[l] Smiths Qu[r] landing & so up Piscatua Creek to the Old Mill from thence along the Road to Harpers Ordinary from thence to Coll Taylors Qu[r] landing beginning the fifth day of Decemb[r] & to finish by the fifteenth day of Jan[y] & make their return as the Law directs.

Ordered that William Covington Thom[s]: Dun James Dix or any two of them procession Every persons land in their precinct beginning at Mathews Bridge from thence to the Road and down the Road to Ellotts old field from thence to y[e] head of the Dragon and down the Dragon to a branch below Jam[s]: Finneys from thence up the s[d] branch to Harpers Ordinary & so along the Road to Matthews bridge beginning the tenth day of Decemb[r] & finish by the last day of Jan[y] and make their return as the law directs.

Ordered that William Carroll William St John & Jeremy Shepherd or any two of them procession Every persons land in their precinct beginning between the two branches of y[e] Dragon from thence up to the Main Road that divides Essex County from King & Queen beginning the twelfth day of Decemb[r] and to finish by the last day of Jan[y] & make their return as the Law directs.

Ordered that William Dun, John Ferguson & William Gatewood or any two of them procession Every persons land in their precinct beginning at Hales Bridge from thence down the Road to the Long Reach Road from thence to the head of Fishers Mill Swamp & down the Swamp to Matthews Bridge from thence along the Road to the Old Mill from thence up the Swamp to Hales Bridge beginning the tenth day of November & to finish by the last day of y[e] same month and to make their return as the Law directs.

Ordered that James Ferguson John Croxon George Wright or any two of them procession Every persons land in their precinct [beginning] at Hales Bridge from thence to the Long Reach Road from thence up ye Road to the dividing line of ye Countys from thence to the head of Piscatua Swamp & so down the Swamp to Hales Bridge beginning the fifteenth day of Novemb^r & to finish by the last day of ye same month and to make their return as the Law directs.

[3]   [1739 Processioning]
Ordered that James Jones Gabriel Jones & Benjamin Johnson or any two of them procession Every persons land in their precinct beginning at Hardees Ferry on Hoskins Creek and so down each creek to the River beginning the twentieth day of Novemb^r & to finish by the twentieth day of Decemb^r & to make their return as the Law directs.

Ordered that James Gatewood Thom^s St John & Thom^s Moor or any two of them procession Every persons land in their precinct between the Little Ferry on Hoskins Creek & Piscatua Ferry & up to Boughans Mill & so up to Whites Run Bridge beginning the twenty second day of Novemb^r and to finish by the twenty second day of Decemb^r and to make their return as the law directs.

Ordered that David Scott Jno: Allen & Thom^s Burnett or any two of them procession Every persons land in their precinct between Boughans Mill & so across to Wareings Mill and so up to Hales Bridge & so across to Wareings Mill Swamp beginning the twenty sixth day of Novemb^r & to finish by the twenty fourth day of Decemb^r & make their return as the law directs.

Ordered that Joseph Reeves Jno: Gatewood & Nicholas Pamplett or any two of them procession Every persons land in their precinct between Hales Bridge & Wareings Mill Swamp up to the dividing line of Essex County from King & Queen County beginning the twenty eighth day of Novemb^r and to finish by the first day of Jan^y & to make their return as the law directs.

Ordered that Isaac Scandrett Robert Coleman & Jam^s Custis or any two of them procession Every persons land in ye Mill Neck from John Armstrongs & so across to William Greenhills beginning the third day of Decemb^r & to finish by the twelfth day of Jan^y & make their return as the law directs.

Ordered that Benjamin Wagginer Thom^s: Davis & William Greenhill or any two of them procession Every persons land between John Armstrongs & William Greenhills & Major Warings Mill & so across to Henry Tandys beginning the fifth day of Decemb^r & to finish by ye fifteenth day of Jany to make their return as the law directs.

Ordered that Henry Tandy John Sears & Henry Padgett procession Every persons land in their precinct Between Major Wareings Mill & Henry Tandys so up to Charles Allen from thence to M^r: James Rennoles beginning ye tenth day of Decemb^r & to finish by ye last day of Jan^y & make their return as ye law directs.

Ordered that Richd Upshaw John Watkins & Thomas Coleman or any two of them procession Every persons land in the upper precinct to King & Queen beginning the twelfth day of Decemb^r & to finish by the last day of Jan^y & to make their return as the law directs.

        Sign^d
        William Philips
        John Robinson Church Wardens
        Jn° Vass Clk to ye Vestry

Truly Registered p^r Jn°: Vass Clk to ye Vestry

****

[4] [1739 Processioning]
At a Vestry held for the parish of South Farnham at John Evans Aprill ye 8th 1740

The Honour^ble John Robinson Esqr
Mr William Covington }
Capt William Dangerfield } Church Wardens

Capt Nicholas Smith Capt Alexander Parker
M.^r: Abraham Mountague M.^r: John Vass

Ordered that the Returns made by the Processioners be truly registered in the Vestry Book and to be Examined by the Vestry to See that they be rightly entered any time within six months after ye date hereof.

Sign.^d
William Dangerfield
William Covington   Church Wardens

In Compliance to an order of Vestry dated the 25th day of July 1739 It was ordered that Abraham Mountague Rice Jones & John Bush should procession the land in the lower precinct and wee the subscribers herein have proceeded as followeth vizt

On the 15th day of Novemb.^r: wee procession.^d the County line between M.^r. Christopher Curtis & M.^r: Rice Jones and ye line between William Buford & William Fletchers Orphans & the line between Charles Medearis and William Baskett and the line between William Baskett and the line that formerly belonged to Edward Pendergrass and ye line between John Paces Orphans and Capt Alexander Parker William Broocks and John Goar in Company and the line between John Massey and Diana Stockley William Broocks in Company and the line between John Massey and John Bush and the line between John Bush and Capt William Mountague and the line between Capt William Mountague and Abraham Mountague John Massey in Company.

On the 16th day wee processioned the line between John Bush & Abraham Mountague and the line between Thomas Dean and Abraham Mountague and the line between Capt Alexander Parker & Thomas Dean and ye line between Thom.^s Dean & John Bush, Thomas Dean Thomas Pain and William Davis in Company and the line between Capt Alexander Parker & John Bush and ye line between Cap 'Alexander Parker and Dianna Stockley William Davis in Company and ye line between Capt Alexander Parker and William Baskett and ye line between Capt Alexander Parker and Rebeckah Duckworth William Davis in Company and the line between Capt Alexander Parker and Capt William Mountague.

[5]   [1739 Processioning]
William Davis and Thomas Pain in Company.

On the 17th day Wee processioned the line between Capt Alexander [Parker] William Montague and John Massey Thomas Pain & John Massey in Company; and the line between William Richeson & Abraham Montague and the line between William Richeson and John Massey John Massey in Company and the line between William Richeson and Thomas Shelton Thomas Shelton in Company and the line between Thomas Shelton & John Jones and the line between John Massey & Thomas Salt and the line between Thomas Shelton & John Massey and the line between John Massey and Thomas Clark John Masey & Thomas Clark and Thomas Shelton in Company and the line between John Paces Orphans & Diana Stockley and the line between John Paces Orphans and John Massey Thomas Clark & John Massey in Company and ye line between John Bush & Diana Stockley Thomas Thomson in Company.

On the 24th day Wee procession^d the line between M^r: Rice Jones & Rebeckah Duckworth & ye line betwen M^r: Rice Jones & Capt Alexander Parker John Jones & William Davis in Company.

On the 27th day of the afores^d month Wee procession^d the line between M^r: Joshua Frys Qu^r: Land & Thom^s Pain M^r: Joshua Fry & Thom^s Pain in Company, and the line between Thom^s Pain and Abraham Mountague M^r: Joshua Fry & Ralph Shelton in Company and ye line between Capt William Mountague and Thom^s Pain Thomas Paine in Company with us.
                                        Abrah^m Mountague
                                        John his HH mark Bush

Wee the subscribers in pursuance to an order of Vestry dated the 26th day of July 1739 have processioned the several persons lands within our precinct Viz^t: The land belonging to Pains orphans is processioned in the presence of James Callicoat and Andrew Hardee. Andrew Hardees land processioned in the presence of Thomas Smith & Andrew Hardee. William Callicoat land processiond in the presence of Thom^s Smith and Andrew Hardee. Thomas Smith land processiond in the presence of Andrew Hardee & Thomas Smith. The land call^d Old Webbs not processioned for want of some body to shew the line. Hugh Williams land processiond in the presence of Andrew Hardee & Charles Burnett. The Lands of William Broocks. Thom^s: Williams is processioned round in the presence of Samuell Broocks & Thom^s Williams but no lines to divide ye same.

[6]   [1739 Processioning]
John Philips land is processioned in the presence of Thomas Williams & John Philips.
Bibby Bush land processioned in the presence of John Broocks & Bibby Bush.
Peter Mitchels land procession^d in the presence of Jno Evans & Peter Mitchell & Peter Mitchell.
The land of M^r: Peter Godfrey procession^d in the presence of John Evans.
The lands belonging to the heir of John Goar in the possession of Richd Johnson and ye lands of John Young wee have processioned round but finding no line to divide the s^d land and ye Heir of ye sd Goar being in her minority have referred making a dividing line between the proprietors till further proceedings therein.
John Broocks land is procession^d in ye presence of Thom^s Williams Hugh Williams & Sam^{ll} Broocke.
The line between Capt William Beale & John Smith not procession^d there being a dispute and no body to shewth the line.
The land belonging to John Webb processioned in the presence of Richd Johnson & Jno: Evans: only a line between ye sd Webb & Evans not yet setled.
The line between Capt Samuel Peachey & Capt Joshua Fry not procession^d being desired by a note to delay it til the Holy days are over which request wee cannot comply with being limitted by the order of Vestry.

        John Webb
        John Young
        Hugh Williams

Pursuant to an order of vestry bearing Date the 25th day of July 1739 Wee the subscribers have processioned and renewed all the Landmarks within our precincts as followeth

The line of Jeremiah Shepherd & Daniel Dobyns in the presence of Rich^d

Covington & George Newbill.
The line of Elizabeth Cole and George Newbill in the presence of George Newbill & James Newbill.
The line of Richd Covington and Jeremiah Shepherd and Jeremiah Shepherd Junr the line of Richd Jones in the presence of Thomas Howerton.
The line of James Newbill, the line of William Covington & Samuell Coats in the presence of William Covington Junr and James Newbill.
The line of Thomas Coleman Sam^{ll} Coats & Capt Armstead in the presence of William Bohannan.
The line of William Crow in the presence of Thomas Parron.

[7]   [1739 Processioning]
All the aforesaid Lines have been renewed according to the ancient bounds but through the neglect of several of the proprietors within the s^d precincts their lands have not been processioned according to the intent and strict letter of the Law. Given under our hands this 28th: day of January 1739.

        William Carroll
        William St John
        Jeremiah Shepherd

Pursuant to an order of Vestry of South Farnham Parish bareing date the 25th day of July 1739 Wee the Subscribers on the 2d of Jan^y [1740] processioned the Lands a[s] followeth Viz^t:

The Ordinary Land James Webbs Land James Dix land & William Covingtons land in ye presence of James Finney John Gresham Richd Brown on the fourth day of January wee processioned ye lands of Richd Brown ye land of William Matthews dec^d and Land of George Turner & ye land of James Turner in the presence of Richd Brown George Turner & James Turner.

On the 5th day of the said instant wee processioned the Line between Edward Marlow & Thomas Newbill the s^d Marlow being absent wee proceeded no further for want of attendance to shew us ye lines & very bad weather.

Thomas Dun
James Dix

Pursuant to an order of Vestry held for Southfarnham Parish the 25th: of July 1739 Wee the Subscribers have processioned ye lands of the several persons in our precinct as followeth

Decemb^r ye 3rd Wee began & processioned the lands of the Betty Fitsjeffries & Thomas Cooper present Thomas Fitsjeffries.

The 8th Wee processioned ye lands of Dan^ll Dobyns John Dobyns Robert James Jane Roberts of George Coleman and of Richd Bush (at Smiths Mill) present Robert James John Dobyns & Martha Hoskins.

The 15th: Wee Processioned the land of John Evans and of Charles Breedlove present Charles Breedlove Thom^s: Cox & Simon Sacry.

The 18th: Wee processioned ye lands of Richd Bush of John Hoskins of Bibby Bush of Catharine Cole & of John Treble present Jno: Hoskins John Treble & William Treble.

[8]   [1739 Processioning]
The 28th Wee processioned the lands of John Hardee Robert Leverit John Davis Hall & Thomas Williamson Junr present John Davis Hall & Thomas Williamson jun^r.

The 29th Wee processioned the lands of Thomas Edmondson and of William Hamor the s^d Edmondson & Hamor present.

January 7th Wee processioned ye lands of Benjamin Fisher and William Gatewood present Thom^s: Williamson jun^r and John Davis Hall.

The 8th Wee processioned the lands of John Davis Charles Wilson John Page John Evans jun^r Thom^s Kidd William Williamson Thomas Williamson & of Robert Acres present Thomas Edmondson Jno: Davis Hall William Hamor & John Roden.

The 9th Wee processioned the land of Robert Leverit jun^r and of John Cox (all but the dividing line between which they do agree to have sett[l]ed themselves) present William Hamor.

The 12th: Wee processioned William Bowlwares lands present James Attkins & William Edmondson.

       Dan^ll Dobyns
       Richd Bush
       John Hardee

On Tuesday ye 20th day of Novemb^r Wee processioned the Line between M^r: Joshua Frys Qu^r land & Thomas Broocks John Bird in Company. Then ye line between Capt William Beale & James Medley, John Medley in Company. Then ye line between ye Gleab & John Vass and ye line between Abraham Mountague and James Medley the Rever^d Mr Philips & John Medley in Company.

On Wednesday ye 21st Wee processioned ye Line between James Medley & M^r. Frys Quarter Land & ye line between James Medley & Abraham Mountague, John Medley Abraham Mountague in Company, then ye line between John Vass & Capt Beale Land.

On Thursday ye 22^d [we] processioned ye line between James Medley Senior & Capt William Beals Land & Joseph Pattersons land & John Vass land James Medley Senr & James Medley jun^r in Company.

Then the Line between ye Widdow Smith & M^r. Heards Land James Medley William Langhorn in Company.

Then the line between John Boughton & Joseph Pattersons land & the line between M^r: Heard & John Boughton and Joshua Boughton in Company of William Langhorn & James Medley.

Novemb^r 27th Processioned the line between Capt Beale and M^r: Corbin & ye line between M^r: Corbin & M^rs: Adams in Company of Jacob Abbott & William Yarington.

[9]   [1739 Processioning]
Decembr ye 1st processioned the line between M^r: Bird and John Boughton in Company of Jam^s Callicoat and Richd Marshall.

        Joshua Boughton
        John his B mark Boughton

Pursuant to an order of Vestry held for Southfarnham Parish July ye 15th [25th] 1739 Wee the Subscribers have processioned the lands of the several persons in our precinct as followeth

Novemb^r ye 20th Wee began & processioned the lands of William Broocke & Henry Crutcher, present Henry Johnson and Richd Crutcher.
The 22nd: Wee processioned the lands of Nathaneel Newbill and M^r: James Webb, present John Burnet.
The 23rd Wee processioned the lands of John Chaney Capt Nicholas Smith Nicholas Smith jun^r & Capt Francis Smith, present Capt Francis Smith & Edward Bomer.
The 27th Wee processioned the lands of Thomas Hastie and Jeremiah Shepherd jun^r: present Edward Bomer Jeremy Shepherd John St John & Thomas Simes.
The 28th: Wee processioned the lands of William Chaney Edward Bomer a parcell of land of Dan^ll Dobyns and the land of William Dobyns deceas^d present Dan^ll Dobyns Edward Bomer William Chaney & John St John.
The 29th Likewise Wee processioned the land of James Hipkings dec^d and the land of Henry Hudson dec^d pres^t Henry Johnson.

        John Cheney
        Nicholas Smith Junr
        Thomas Broocke

Pursuant to an order of Vestry dated ye Twenty fifth day of July 1739 Wee the Subscribers to whome ye said order was directed to procession has proceeded as followeth vizt

William Gatewood land processioned.
Henry Reeves Land processioned.
Amey Bakers Land processioned.
Patience Gatewood Land processioned.
James Gatewood Land processioned.

Capt William Dangerfield Land processioned in the presence of Mr Isaac Scandrett & John Bates.
M^r: Isaac Scandrett Land processioned in ye presence of Cap William Dangerfield and John Bates.
Thomas Burk Land processioned.
William Fretwell Land processioned.
Ann Reeves land processioned.
Acquile Blaxton Land processioned.
Gabriel Jones Land processioned.
John Picket Land processioned.
Part of John Boughan Land processioned.
Part of James & Thom^s St Johns Land processioned.

[10]   [1739 Processioning]
The Line between John Boughan and James & Thomas St John not processioned by ye reason— they could show none.

       James Gatewood
       Thom^s Moore
       Thom^s: St John

In obedience to an order of Vestry held for Southfarnham Parish ye 25th day of July 1739. Wee the Subscribers have processioned the following persons Lands (Viz^t)

The Land of John Armstrong peaceably processioned, present Matthew Wellman. The Land of William Greenhill peaceably processioned. The Land of Christopher Beverley processioned by Matthew Wellman, present Benjamin Allen. The Land of Ga[b]reil Fitsimmons peaceably procession^d, present Thomas Evans. The Land of Benjamin Wagginer peaceably procession^d, present James Wagginer. The Land of Thomas Waring jun^r peaceably processioned, present Francis Jones. The Land of Francis Jones peaceably processioned, present Thom^s Waring jun^r. The Land of Thomas Evans peaceably processioned. The Land whereon John Seares liveth not processioned by reason that he said it was orphans Land. The Land of Thomas Davis the upper part not procession^d by reason that it joyns on Sears Land the lower part peaceably processioned. The Land of Daniel Daley peaceably processioned, present Matthew Wellman.

Witness our hands this 5th: day of January 1739.
                           Benjamin Wagginer
                           Thomas Davis
                           William Greenhill

Pursuant to an order of Vestry of Southfarnham Parish Dated July ye 25th 1739. Wee the Subscribers have processioned the Lands according to the precincts in the s^d order mentioned as followeth Viz^t.

Decemb^r ye 10th 1739 Wee processioned the Land of William Mitchell and also the land formerly belonging to John Dyke Deceas^d and also ye land of Richd Cauthorn which he purchased of the s^d Dyke according to ye reputed bounds thereof present Thomas Johnson Andrew Hardee William Mitchell and Henry Faulkner.

Decemb^r ye 12th: 1739. Wee processioned the Land of Thomas Cauthorn on the southside of ye main Road by Col^l Robinsons Quarter & the Land of Thomas Johnson and the Land of Isaac Mitchell lying on the South Side of ye said Road and ye Land of James Profnall & John Minter and John Cammell according to the reputed bounds thereof, present Isaac Mitchell & John Cammell.

Decemb^r ye 10th 1739 Wee processioned ye Land of Richd Williams Godfrey Piles and Joseph Anderson Deceas^d lying on the South Side of the afores^d Main Road & also ye Land of Ludo Piles & Jo^s Evans jun^r according to the reputed bounds thereof, present Samue^{ll} Piles. Given under our hands this 19th day of March 1739.
                           John Evans Junr
                           Ludo Piles

[11]   [1739 Processioning]
Pursuant to an Order of Vestry of Southfarnham Parish bearing Date the 25th day of July 1739 Wee the Subscribers have processioned the Lands in our precinct as followeth. (Viz^t)

The line between Henry Young & John Young processioned in the presence of John Young & Nathaneel Pendleton. The Line between

Henry Young & Williamson Young processiond in the presence of John Young & Nathaneel Pendleton. The line between ye Hon ^{ble}: John Robinson Esqr and Henry Young processioned in ye presence of John Young & Nathan^{ll} Pendleton. The line between William Lowry Gen^t: & Henry Young procession^d in the presence of John Young & Nathanee^{ll} Pendleton. The Line between the Honble: John Robinson Esqr & James Webb processioned in presence of Col^l John Robinson & Henry Pearcey. The line Between the Honble: John Robinson Esqr and Eliza^{bth} Owen Processioned in the presence of Col^l John Robinson, Elizabeth Owen, Henry Pearcey & Parrott Hardee. The Line between ye Honorable John Robinson Esqr: and Ann Williams processioned in the presence of Col^l John Robinson Henry Pearcey and Parrot Hardy. The line between Ann Williams & James Webb processiond in ye presence of Henry Pearcey and Parrott Hardee. The line [between] M^{rs}: Elizabeth Clayton & Elizabeth Owen procession^d in the presence of George Clayton & Parrott Hardee. And ye rest of the Lands in the precinct of the Subscribers remains unprocessioned for want of some one to shew them to.

Decemb^r: ye 28th 1739   Henry Young
　　　　　　　　　　　　　　　　Jam^s: Webb
　　　　　　　　　　　　　　　　John Webb

In obedience to an order of Vestry bearing date July ye 25th 1739 Wee have processiond all the lands in the precincts as followeth.

The line Between Col^l John Tayloe & Benjamin Fisher. The line between Col^l Jno: Tayloe & James Fisher. The line between Capt Peachey & James Fisher in the presence of Crispen Shelton. The line between Capt Peachey & Thom^s Williamson jun^r and ye line between Capt Peachey & John Williamson in the presence of Crispen Shelton. The line between Capt Peachey & John Tyler in the presence of Crispen Shelton & William Tyler. The line between Capt Philip Jones & John Tyler in the presence of Crispen Shelton and William Tyler. The line between Capt Peachey and ye land that was formerly Ann Prices. The line between James Boughan & William Tyler. The line between James Boughan & Capt Philip Jones in ye presence of William Tyler. The line between Capt Peachey & Jno: Tyler Quarter Land and Capt Peachey & William Tyler in the presence of Crispen Shelton.

[12]   [1739 Processioning]

The line between Capt Peachey & James Turner in the presence of Crispen Shelton. The line between Jame[s] Turner & William Matthews. The line between James Turner & Richd Cooper in ye presence of George Turner. The line between James Turner & William Cooper in ye presence of George Turner. The line between James Turner and John Page in ye presence of William Cooper. The line between James Turner and John Williamson in the presence of William Cooper. The line between William Cooper and John Page. The line between William Cooper & Robert Patten. The line between Robert Patten & John Davis. The line between John Williamson Junr: & Abraham St John in the presence of John Davis & John Roden. The line between John Williamson Junr and Mary Brisendine in the presence of John Davis & John Roden. The line between Mary Brisendine & William Williamson jun^r in the presence of John Williamson. The line between Thomas Williamson and Robert Ackres. The line between Robert Ackres & John Cox in the presence of Robert Ackres. The line between M^r: John Baylor and John Cox in the presence of Robert Ackres. The line between John Cox & Robert Leveril Junr: not agreed on Wee went no farther then to John Cox and Leverit Corner Tree by the Reason Richd Bush and John Hardee had done all from that Corner to the lower end of our precinct. Given under our hands.   James Turner
                                James Boughan

In obedience to an order of Vestry made July ye 25th: 1739 Wee the Subscribers being appointed to procession the land between Hails Bridge and Warings Mill Swamp up to the Dividing line of Essex County from King & Queen.

Decemb^r ye 11th 1739 Procession^d a line between John Hale and Richd Compton, also a line between John Hale and Mary Dix, also a line between Richd Compton & Mary Dix, present John Hale William Dix & Richd Compton.

Decemb^r: ye 14th: 1739 Present John Allen John Hunt Thom^s Gatewood and Richd Compton William Dix Thomas Bell Processioned between John Haile and Richd Compton and between Mary Dix & Richd Compton and between Thomas Gatewood and Richd Compton and between John

Hunt & William Dix & between Jno: Allen & John Hunt & between John Hunt & Thom^s: Bell.

Decemb^r ye 15th: 1739 Present Capt William Roan Isaac Gatewood John Gatewood jun^r: Processioned a line between Isaac Gatewood & John Gatewood jun^r: & between Jno Gatewood and Nicholas Pamplin & between Thomas Johnson and Nicholas Pamplin & between Capt William Roan and Thomas Johnson.

Decemb^r ye 27th: 1739 Present John Hunt William Dix William Bradberry George Moody Capt William Roan John Latane & Edwd Davis William Hull. Processioned a line between John Hunt and George Moody & between George Moody

[13]   [1739 Processioning]
George Moody & John Allen & between William Dix and Jane Gorden & between Richd Johnson and William Dix and between John Allen & William Hull and between James Gatewood & Mary Dix and between John Hale & James Gatewood and between Capt William Roan & Jane Gorden and between Capt William Roan and Richd Johnson.

Decemb^r ye 29th 1739 Present Capt William Roan processioned a line between M^{rs}: Mary Lattane & Capt William Roan between Jeremy Upshaw & Capt William Roan and between Roberts Orphans & Nicholas Pamplin and between Capt William Roan & Nicholas Pamplin and between Capt William Roan & John Gatewood & between John Gatewood and Nicholas Pamplin.

Decemb^r ye 31st: 1739 Present Capt William Roan & Richard Gatewood Processioned a line between Edward Davis and Theodrick Bland and a line between John Gatewood and Theodrick Bland.

The land of Gregory Smith & ye land of Robert Price and the dividing lines of Richd Johnson & William Hull and James Gatewood not processioned for want of ye line shewd to us.

John his I mark Gatewood
Nicholas Pamplin

In Pursuance of an order of Vestry of Southfarnham Parish Dated July ye 25th: 1739 Wee the Subscribers have processioned the lands as followeth.

The line between James Boughan & John Smith peaceably processioned in the presence of John Boughan. Also between John Farguson & John Smith in presence of James Boughan. Also between Jonathan Jones & Henry Purkins in presence of James Boughan & Henry Brown. Also between the s^d Jones & George Radford in the presence of Henry Purkins and Andrew Evitt. Also between Henry Purkins & John Boughan in the presence of Sarah Boughan & Cary Purkins. Also the line of Andrew Evitt & Abner Boughan & also the line of the s^d Evitt and George Radford. Also the line between Philip Jones Gen^t & the s^d Evitt & between ye s^d Jones and George Radford & between the s^d Philip Jones and John Brown and between the s^d Philip Jones & William Gatewood in the presence of John Brown. Also the line between M^r: Skelton and Richd Jones in the presence of Francis Jones. But the line between Mary Padgett & M^r: Skelton not processioned for want of persons to shew the line. Also the line between John Farguson & John C[r]oxton and between Henry Boughan & ye s^d Croxton and between the s^d Croxton and Francis Brown in the present of John [Croxton] and Thom^s Croxton & Henry Boughan. Also the line between Thomas Younger & James Edmondson and Francis Brown & William Gatewood in the presence of John C[r]oxton. Also the line between James Edmondson and Mr Farish in the presence of John Edmondson. Also the line between William Gatewood and Richard Jones in the presence of Ambrose Jones.

[14]   [1739 Processioning]
Also the line between Mary Padgett & James Edmondson in presence of John Edmondson & Ambrose Jones. Also the line between William Dunn and James Skelton and ye line between James Boughan & the s^d Skelton in the presence of Ambrose Jones and Isaac St John. Also the line between Thomas Dunn & Mary Padgett and between William Dunn and the s^d Padgett in the presence of John Dunn and Ambrose Jones. Also the line between Wm Dun & James Skelton & the line between Ja^s. Boughan and the s^d Skelton in the presence of Ambrose Jones & Isaac St John. Also the line Between John Tyler and William Dunn in the presence of the s^d Ambrose Jones & Isaac St John.

William Dunn
John Fargeson
William Gatewood

Pursuant to an order of Vestry held for Southfarnham parish the 15th day of July 1739. Wee the Subscribers have processioned the lands of the Severall persons within our precincts as follows. (Viz^r)

Decemb^r ye 11th 1739 Wee processioned the land of Mr John Evans Junr in presence of ye s^d Evans & John Souls. Wee processioned the land of M^r: James Jones in presence of the s^d Jones and M^r: John Evans Junr. Wee processioned the land of M^r: Benjamin Johnson in presence [of] s^d Johnson & M^r: John Evans Junr. Wee processioned the land of M^{rs}. Suckey Edmondson an orphan of M^r. John Edmondson Deceas^d: the Bounds of which s^d land was Shewd by M^r: Gabriel Jones who acted in behalf of the s^d orphan present M^r: John Evans jun^r. Wee processioned the land of M^r: Gabriel Jones that is within our precinct that he purchased of M^r: John Pickett present the s^d Jones & John Evans jun^r.

14th Wee processioned the Land of M^r: Peter Godfrey in presence of the s^d Godfrey & William Smith. The land in our precinct belonging to the Orphans of the Honble Man Page Esqr: deceas^d: not processioned by us because no person appeared to shew us the bounds there of. The land in our precinct in possession of Thomas Hardy not processioned because no person appeared to shew us the bounds. The Land of John Chamberlain not processioned because no person appeared to shew us the bounds of the said land. The land of M^r. G Jones wch he purchased of Peter Trible Dec^d not proc^d because no person appear^d to shew us the bounds of the same except one line from Piscataway Ferry Road that leads to Hardys Ferry and So down the s^d line to a Gum [tree] standing near the head of a branch, present ye s^d Jones and Maurice Knight. The Land of Thomas Games not processioned because no person appeared to shew us the bounds of the s^d land. The Land of William Smith not processioned because no person appeared to shew us the bounds thereof. No other person haveing Lands within our precinct that Wee ar[e] Sensible of. Given under our hands this 15th: day of Decemb^r 1739.

James Jones
Benjamin Johnson

Gabriel Jones

[15]   [1739 Processioning]
In obedience to an Order of Vestry bareing date July ye 25th 1739 Wee the Subscribers being appointed to procession the land between Boughans Mill & Wareings Mill and to Hales Bridge.

Decemb^r: ye 17th Processioned the land of John Hale jun^r, present Richd Compton Samuell Shaw. Processioned the Land of William Allen, present Thomas Gatewood Herbert Wagginer Thom^s: Bell. Processioned the land of Thomas Bell, present William Allen Thomas Gatewood Herbert Wagginer. Processioned all the land of Thomas Gatewood & Richard Compton in our precinct below the Road that goeth from Hails bridge to Warings old Mill. Processioned the Land of Henry Harper present Samuel Shaw John Burnett Joseph Burnett. Processioned the land of John Pette present John Burnett Joseph Burnett. Processioned the Land of Peter Kemp only the lower part wee could not find the line, present Samuell Shaw.

The 20th: Processioned the land of William Meader present Harbert Wagginer. Processioned the land of Susanna Meader present William Meader Harbert Wagginer. Processioned the land of Harbert Wagginer present William Meader William Allen. Processioned the land of Thomas Meader present William Meader William Allen David Faulkner.

Decemb^r: ye 20th Processioned the land of Zacharias Allen present Thomas Meader David Faulkner William Meader Harbert Wagginer. Processioned the land of Samuell Waggener present Thomas Meader William Allen William Meader Harbert Wagginer.

Processioned the land of Henry Reeves Joyning to the land of Samual Wagginer present William Allen Thomas Meader David Faulkner William Meader.

The 22^d: Processioned the land of John Burnett and Joseph Burnett present David Scott John Attwood. The land of George Reeves is not processioned because no body came to shew the bounds. The Land of

John Allen Joyning to the land of George Reeves is not processioned because the land of the s^d Reeves is not. The land of Hugh Willsons not processioned no body came to shew the bounds. The Land of Nathaneell Pendleton not processioned no body came to shew the bounds. Given under our hands this 24th of Decemb^r 1739.

John Allen
Thomas Burnett

Pursuant to an order of Southfarnham parish the 25th day of July 1739: Wee the Subscribers being appointed Processioners of the upper precinct of the afores^d: parish did on the 28th: day of January 1739 Begin at a corner of M^r: James Rennolds and being accompanied with the sd James Rennolds William Rennolds John Rennolds

[16]   [1739 Processioning]
Robert Rennolds William Waller John Hill & William Sthreshley, Wee proceeded on a line between the s^d James Rennolds and William Sthreshley to the Road Swamp, thence to a Corner of John Hills land, thence along a line between the s^d John Hill & James Rennolds to a Corner of M^rs: Hannah Sthreshley thence along a line between the s^d Hannah Sthreshley & James Rennolds to a corner of the s^d James Rennolds Hannah Sthreshley & Hannah Upshaw thence along a line between the s^d Hannah Upshaw & Hannah Sthreshley to a Corner of William Wallers land thence along a line between the s^d Waller & Hannah Sthreshley to Horskins Swamp.

And on the 29th: day Wee met at a Corner of the said William Waller and Hannah Upshaw & being accompanied with the said Waller and Forrest Upshaw. William Gatewood William Rennolds John Rennolds Robert Rennolds John Hill William Sthreshley and proceeded a line Between William Waller & Hannah Upshaw and ye s^d Waller & Richard Upshaw to William Gatewoods land, thence along a line between ye s^d: Waller & Gatewood to Hoskin's Swamp thence along a line between the s^d Gatewood & Richd Upshaw to a corner of Forrist Upshaw thence along a line between ye s^d Forrest Upshaw & William Gatewood to Horskins Swamp, thence along Forrest Upshaws line to Thomas Colemans line thence wee went round the s^d Colemans land thence along a line between

John Watkins & William Rennolds to Daniel Sweleivans land thence along a line between ye s^d Swileivan & Watkins and also two lines between ye s^d Swelervan & James Rennolds.

And on ye 30th day Wee met at a Corner of William Rennolds and Thomas Colemans and being accompanied with William Rennolds James Rennolds John Rennolds Robert Rennolds John Upshaw Forrest Upshaw John Hill & William Sthreshley wee proceeded on a line of William Rennolds to a corner of Forrest Upshaws thence along a line of Forrest Upshaw to the s^d Colemans line, thence along two lines between the s^d William Rennolds & Forrest Upshaw to a corner of Richard Upshaws land thence along a line between the s^d William Rennolds and Richd Upshaw to a corner of the s^d Richd Upshaw & Hannah Upshaw thence along a line between ye s^d Richd Upshaw and Hannah Upshaw to William Wallers line thence a line between ye s^d Hannah Upshaw & William Rennolds, and finished Howells land & Holts land & Absalom Wells land not processioned by reason there was no body to shew ye lines. Given under our hands this 30th day of January 1739.

> Richd Upshaw
> John Watkins
> Thom^s: Coleman

In obedience to an order of Vestry of Southfarnham parish dated July ye 25th: 1739 Wee the Subscribers have performed the processioning according to order as followeth January ye 1st Processioned the land of Henry Tandy in the presence of Robert Seayres Francis Jones William Bradbery

January ye 3rd Processioned the Land of M^r: William Fantilleroy in the presence of Robert Seayres Henry Harper John Billips.

Jan ye 4th Processioned the land of Capt. Francis Smith shewed us by James Harper in behalf of the s^d Smith in the presence of John Chick.

Processioned the land of Capt Thom^s Belfield shewd us by George Coleman in behalf of ye s^d: Belfield in the presence of John Chick.

[17]   [1739 Processioning]
Wee could not procession the land of Capt Thomas Sthreshley Deceas^d being Orphans land. Processioned the land of Mrs Hannah Sthreshley in the presence of George Coleman John Cheek James Harper. Processioned the Land of John Hill in the presence of John Cheek George Coleman James Harper.

Jany ye 5th: Processioned the land of Daniell Sillivant in the presence of Leonard Hill Thom^s: Graves. Processioned the Land of Edward Webb in the presence of Robert Seayres Charles Clark.

January ye 7th: Processioned the Bounds between Henry Padgett & Francis Padgett in the presence of John Padgett Junr: & William Woolbanks.

Jany ye 11th Processioned the reputed bounds between Francis Padgett & Nichilas Lefon and likewise between John Padgett & ye s^d Lefon in ye presence of John Padgett Junr: William Woolbanks.

Given under our hands January ye 20th 1739.
                                    Henry Tandy
                                    John Seayres
                                    Henry Pagett

Novemb^r ye 15th 1739 in Pursuance to a Order of vestry dated ye 25th day of July Wee the Processioners began and processioned the lands as followeth:

Processioned the line between James Boughan and Thomas Barker in the presence of John Smith and Daniell Hodghill.
The line Between Thomas Barker & James Farguson in the presence of John Smith & John Ball.
The line Between James Farguson & John Croxton in the presence of John Smith & John Ball.
The line between Capt William Ayllott & Thomas Younger in the presence of John Ball & Thomas Wodlenton*: the lines between Capt William Ayllott and Richd Jones in the presence of Benjamin Jones Thomas Wodlenton & William Cox.
The 19th of this Instant processioned the line between Col^l George

Braxton & Joseph Reeves in ye presence of John Ball & Francis Boughan. The line between Jo^s Reeves and Rob 'Price in presence of Jn .^o Ball & Francis Boughan.

The 26: of this Instant processioned the line between Joseph Reeves & John Ball in the presence of John Lumpkin & Samuell Allen.

The line between Thomas Harwood deceas^d: and John Ball in the presence of John Lumpkin and Samuell Allen. The line between John Ball and Thos Martin in presence of John Lumpkin & Saml. Allen.

The line between Col^l George Braxton and John Ball in the presence of John Lumpkin & Samuel Allen.

The line between John Ball & Maddam Latane in the presence of John Lumpkin & Samuell Allen.

The line between Samuell Thomson & Thomas Harwood deceas^d in the presence of John Powell and Samuell Allen.

*The line between John Faris & Thos. Younger in ye presence of John Ball and Thom^s Woodlington.

[18]   [1739 Processioning]

The line between William Cox & Samuell Thomson in the presence of Richard Jones.

The lines between William Cox and John Pickett in the presence of Richd Jones & Robert Marsh.

The lines between George Wright & John Pickett in the presence of Richd Jones & William Cox & Robert Ma[r]sh.

The lines between George Wright & William Cox in the presence of Richd Jones & Robert Ma[r]sh.

The lines between Capt William Ayllott & George Wright in the presence of Richd Jones & William Cox.

The line between George Wright & Robert March in the presence of Richd Jones & William Cox.

The line between Richd Jones & Jonathan Clark deceas^d in the presence of William Cox.

The 30th of November Processioned the line between William Cox & Thomas Harwood deceas^d: in the presence of Henry Cox.

The line between Col^l George Braxton & Jno Pickett not to be found till Braxton makes a survey.

The line between Capt William Ayllott & John Farish is defered to be

referred till they can settle it themselves.
The line between Jo^s Reeves & Mad^m Latane in the pres^{ce} of John Ball & Fra^n: Boughan.

George Wright
John Croxton

Pursuant to an order of Vestry of South Farnham parish bareing date the 25th day of July 1739 Wee the Subscribers have processioned the lands in the Mill Neck [as] followeth

Decemb^r: ye 11th 1739 Wee procession^d the lines between John Armstrong & John Bourne & William Dangerfield. Betwixt William Dangerfield & William Gree[n]hill betwixt William Greenhill & Amy Baker. Betwixt Capt Parker & John Bourne all in the presence of William Dangerfield William Greenhill John Bourne Eliz Armstrong also the line betwixt William Greenhill & John Armstrong.

22^d: 1739 Also the line betwixt Capt Parker & William Dangerfield present William Dangerfield. Also ye line Betwixt William Dangerfield & Henry Reeves from ye Mills end to ye River present ye s^d Dangerfield and s^d Reeves. Wee began to procession the line made by Augustine Smith from the Mills end to the back line of Hoskins pattent, but by consent of M^r: Henry Reeves as that line was one of the lines now in dispute there proceedings in that line should be of no effect but stand as before the suit commenced present Henry Reeves William Dangerfield.

All the other lines in our precincts are Orphans, & lines now in Court contended for which wee humbly conceive ought to ly till determined by the Court. Given under our hand this 11th day of March 1739:40.

Isaac Scandrett
Robt Sp: Coleman

[20]   [1739 Processioning]
In Obedience to an order of Essex Court wee the Subscribers being Summon^d & Sworn a Jury to Survey & procession the bounds of Land between M^r: William Lourie on one side and the Honble John Robinson Esqr & Capt Francis Smith on the other side did in Company with Robert

Brooke Surveyor Survey the Bounds which M^r: Lourie Shew^d us for his Land. Beginning at M^r: Henry Youngs uppermost line by the River Side which land was formerly granted to one Soan's and went thence along that line to the said Youngs outermost bounds from whence the s^d Lourie directed the Surveyor to run a NW Course to Piscataway Creek to which Course Col^l Robinson & Capt Smith objected. In Going which line wee saw no marked trees from the end of his line. Capt Francis Smith desired the Surveyor to measure 100 p^o: down the s^d brook to an old marked line to which Richard Cauthorn made oath he had known that for thirty years past a reputed marked line "Between Bush & Boughton as far as the Beaver Dam which wee found marked to Youngs line where was a Live Oak which wee think had been marked for a Corner but blazed out again the said Lourie would not agree this line to be his bounds nor it doth not appear to us a processioned line from the Beaver Dam to Youngs line but finding no other marked line Wee processioned this line for the s^d Louries bounds but for a plainer Description of our proceedings herein Wee refer to the Surveyors platt. Given under our hands & seals this Eleventh day of January Ann^o: Do^m 1739.

        Thomas Edmondson   John Hale jun^r
        William Dunn   Benj^a Fisher
        James Turner   W. Tyler
        John Farguson   Wm Gatewood

        A. Mountague foreman
        Gabriel Jones
        Ben Johnson
        John Young

Copia vera
Esqr Henry Robinson D Cl Cur
Truly registered p^r Jno: Vass Clk to ye Vestry

[20]   [1739 Processioning]
At a Vestry held for South Farnham Parish at John Evans August ye 7th 1740. Present
        The Rever^d: M^r: William Philips
        Capt William Dangerfield } Church Wardens
        M^r: William Covington

Capt Alexander Parker: Capt William Roan
M^r: James Rennolds & John Vass

Then the Gentlemen of the Vestry met to Examine whether the returns made by the Processioners were Justly & truley Entered in the Book appointed by the Vestry for that purpose within the time as the law directs: and do find the s^d returns to be truly Entered.

Sign^d:
Wm: Philips
Wm: Covington
Wm: Dangerfield

Truly registered p^r Jno: Vass Clk to ye Vestry

****

[21]   [1743 Processioning]
At a vestry held for the parish of South Farnham at Piscatua Ferry the 11th day of July 1743, present
    The Revd Wm Philips
    Capt Francis Smith Church Warden
    Capt Alexander Parker Capt Nicholas Smith
    Capt W^m: Dangerfield M^r: W^m: Covington Mr Isaac Scandreth
    M^r: John Vass Mr Henry Young Mr Jam^s Webb

Pursuant to an order of Court for the County of Essex bareing date the 20th day of June 3 anno Domino 1743 where by it is ordered that the Vestry of Each parish within the s^d County divide their parishes into so many precincts as to them shall seem most convenient for processioning every particular persons lands in the several Parishes & appoint the particular times for processioning likewise appoint two intelligent honest freeholders at least of every precinct to see such Processioning perform^d and take & return to ye Vestry an acc^t of Every persons land they shall procession and of the persons present at ye same and what Land in their precincts they shall fail to procession & of the particular reasons of such failure.

This present Vestry do therefore divide the parish of South Farnham into Twenty Precincts and it is ordered that Rice Jones John Bush Thom^s Dean or any two of you procession every persons land in your precinct Beginning at the Lower end of Essex County & run to the Gleab Creek from thence to Capt Joshua Frys Quart 'on the Dragon & make their return as ye law directs beginning the tenth day of Novemb^r and to finish by the last of the Same month and to make their return as the law directs.

Ordered that Joshua Boughton John Boughton and Jam^s Medley or any two of you procession the lands in your precinct Beginning at Capt Frys Quart^r on the Dragon from thence to Joshua Boughtons & so to ye Dragon from thence to M^{rs}: Adams Quarter on the River Side Bowlers Ferry Beginning ye 15th day of November and to finish by the last of the Same month & to make their return as the Law directs.

Ordered that Nicholas Smith jun^r: Thom^s Broocke and Hugh Williams or any two of you procession ye Land in your precinct beginning at Joshua Boughtons & thence up to John Dickes from thence to William Cheney on the Dragon beginning the twentieth day of November and to finish by the twentieth day of Decemb^r and make their return as the Law directs.

[22]   [1743 Processioning]
Ordered that John Webb John Young & Jno: Phillips or any two of you procession the lands in your precinct beginning at Mrs Adams land at ye River Side from thence to Capt Tylers Creek by Jno Hays and so to the Back Road by Thom^s Cauthorn from thence down the s^d Road to Joshua Boughtons beginning the twenty second day of Novemb^r & to finish by the twenty second day of Decemb^r & make their return as the Law directs.

Ordered that John Evans jun^r Sam^{ll} Piles & Nathaneal Pendleton or any two of you procession Every persons land in your precinct beginning at Col^l Robinsons Quarter Land by Thom^s Cauthorns from thence to Jno Dickes from thence down the Mill Swamp to Piscatua Ferry so down the Main Road to Col^l Robinsons Quarter old field beginning the twenty sixth day of November to finish by ye twenty sixth day of Decemb^r and make your return as the Law directs.

Ordered that Capt Richd Tyler M^r: W^m: Lowry & Wmson Young or any two of you procession Every persons land in your precincts beginning at Col¹ Robinsons Quart' Land by Thom⁸: Cauthorns from thence to the Creek where John Philips once liv^d and all the Land between ye River & ye Road to Piscatua Creek beginning the twenty eighth day of Novemb^r & to finish by the first day of January and make your return as the Law directs.

Ordered that Micajah Evans Bibby Bush and Jn° Hardee or any two of you procession Every persons Land in your precinct beginning at W^m: Chaneys on the Dragon from thence to the head of Covingtons Mill Swamp and down the Swamp to Col¹ Tayloes Quart' Landing from thence up the Road by Thom⁸: Williamsons to Wm: Cheneys beginning the third day of Decemb^r & to finish by the twelfth day of January and make their return as ye Law directs.

Ordered that Benjamin Fisher Jam⁸ Fisher & James Boughan jun^r or any two of you procession Every persons Land in your precinct beginning at Col¹ Smiths Qu^r Landing & so up Piscatua Creek to the Old Mill from thence along the Road to Harpers Ordinary from thence down ye branch to the Dragon & to W^m: Cheneys from thence to Col¹ Tayloe's Qu^r Landing beginning the fifth day of Decemb^r and to finish by the fifteenth day of January & make your return as the Law directs.

Ordered that Thoms Dunn Peter Dickason & Richd Brown or any two of you procession Every persons land in your precinct beginning at Mathews Bridge from thence to the Road & down the Road to Elliotts old field from thence to ye head of ye Dragon and down ye Dragon to a branch below Jam⁸ Finnys from thence up the sd branch to Harpers Ordinary & so along ye Road to Mathews Bridge beginning the tenth day of Decembr and to finish by the last day of January & make their return as the law directs.

[23] [1743 Processioning]
Ordered that Richd Gatewood Jam⁸ Newbill & George Newbill or any two of you procession Every persons land in your precinct beginning between the two branches of the Dragon from thence up to the Main Road that divideth Essex County from King & Queen County beginning the twelfth

day of Decembr & to finish by the last day of January and make their return as the law directs.

Ordered that William Dunn John Ferguson & John Edmondson or any two of them procession Every persons Land in their precinct beginning at Hales Bridge from thence down the Road to the Long Reach Road from thence to the head of Fisher's Mill Swamp and down the Swamp to Matthews Bridge from thence along ye Road to ye old Mill from thence up the Swamp to Hales Bridge beginning the tenth day of Novemb^r & to finish by the last day of the same month and to make their return as the Law directs.

Ordered that James Boughan John Croxen & George Wright or any two of them procession Every persons land in their precinct beginning at Hales bridge from thence to ye Long Reach Road from thence up ye Road to ye dividing line of the County from thence to ye head of Piscatua Swamp & so down the Swamp to Hales bridge beginning the fifteenth day of Novemb^r: & to finish by the last day of the same month & to make their return as the Law directs.

Ordered that Jam^s: Jones Gabriel Jones & Thomas Edmondson or any two of them procession Every persons land in their precinct beginning at Hardees Ferry on Hoskins Creek from thence to Piscatua Ferry & so down each creek to the River beginning the twentieth day of Novemb^r & to finish by the twentieth day of Decemb^r & to make their return as ye Law directs.

Ordered that Jam^s: Gatewood Thomas St John & Francis Attwood or any two of them procession Every persons land in their precinct Between ye Little Ferry on Hoskins Creek & Piscatua Ferry & up to Boughans Mill & so up to Whites Run Bridge beginning the twenty second day of Novemb^r & to finish by the twenty second day of Decemb^r & to make their return as the law directs.

Ordered that John Bennett Joseph Bennett & Thomas Bush or any two of them procession Every persons land in their precinct Between Boughans Mill & so across to Warings Mill & so up to Hales Bridge & across to Warings Mill Swamp beginning ye twenty sixth day of Novemb^r & to finish by the twenty fourth of Decemb^r & to make their return as the

Law directs.

Ordered that Joseph Reeves John Gatewood & Nicholas Pamplin or any two of them procession every persons land in their precinct beginning between Hales Bridge & Warings Mill Swamp & up to ye dividing line of Essex County from King & Queen County beginning ye twenty eighth day of Novemb^r & to fnish by ye first day of January and to make their return as the Law directs.

[24]   [1743 Processioning]
Ordered that Benjamin Johnson Joseph Reeves junr & James Reeves procession every persons land in the Mill Neck from John Armstrongs & so across to Wm Greenhills beginning the third day of Decemb^r & to finish by the twelfth day of January & to make their return as the Law directs.

Ordered that Benjamin Wagginer Thom^s. Davis John Brown procession every persons land in their precinct between John Armstrongs & William Greenhills & Major Warrings Mill & so across to Henry Tandys beginning the fifth day of Decemb^r & to finish by the fifteenth day of Jan^y: & to make their return as the Law directs.

Ordered that John Sears Thom^s: Wareing jun^r: & Francis Jones or any two of them procession every persons land in their precinct between Major Wareings Mill & Henry Tandys so up to Charles Walkers from thence to M^r. Jam^s Rennolds beginning the tenth day of Decemb^r. and to finish by ye last day of January & make their return as the Law directs.

Ordered that Richd Upshaw John Wattkins & Thomas Colemon or any two of them procession every persons land in the upper precinct to King & Queen beginning the twelfth day of Decembr: & to finish by ye last day of January & make their return as the Law directs.

         Sign'd
         William Philips:
         Francis Smith CW
Truly Registered p John Vass Clk to ye Vestry

****

[25]   [1743 Processioning]
At a Vestry held for the parish of South Farnham at John Evans Piscataway Ferry Aprill ye 23^d 1744

The Rever^d: William Philips
Capt Francis Smith: Church Warden
Capt Nicholas Smith Capt W^m: Dangerfield M^r: Henry Young
M^r: Jams: Webb M^r: John Vass

Ordered that the returns made by the Processioners be truly registered in the Vestry Book & to be Examin'd over by ye Vestry to see that they be rightly Entered any time within six months after ye Date hereof.

In obedience to an order of vestry held for the parish of South Farnham ye 11th day of July 1743 appointing us ye Subscribers or any two of us to procession ye Several persons lands in y precincts in y s^e order mentioned accordingly wee began on ye 20th of Novemb^r: & processioned ye line between Joshua Boughton and Thom^s Broocke present Henry Cauthorn.

Then processioned ye land of Wm Broocke on ye Dragon present John Broocke.

21st: Then wee processioned the land of Jeremiah Shephard jun^r present Humphrey Davis, also wee processioned ye land of Wm: Cheney present Richd Bresendine.

22^d: Wee processioned the land of Edward Bomar present Peter Bomar. Wee also processioned the land of Wm Dobyns deceas^d present Edward Bomar. Wee also processioned the Land of Wm Dobyns deceas^d present Edward Bomar & John St John.

23^d: Wee procession^d ye land of Henry Crutcher present Henry Johnson & Samuel Smith. Wee also processioned the land of Thom^s Newbil present Henry Johnson & Sam^{ll} Smith. Wee also processioned ye land of Nathanial Newbill present Henry Johnson & Sam^{ll}: Smith. Wee also processioned ye land of Thom^s: Hastie present Henry Johnson & Sam^{ll}

Smith. Wee also processioned ye land of Nichol^s: Smith present Thomas Hastie & Sam^ll: Smith. Wee also processioned the land of John Cheney deceas^d pres^t Richd Johnson & Wm:son Young. Wee also processioned ye land of Jno Lay[?] deceas^d present Richd Johnson & W^m: Mitchell. We also processioned ye land of Jno Smith present Richd Johnson & Henry Johnson.

24th: Wee processioned ye land of Capt Francis Smith present Henry Johnson & Sam^ll: Smith & Henry Crutcher. Wee also processioned ye land of Capt. Nicholas Smith present Capt Francis Smith and Sam^ll: Smith.

Nicholas Smith jun^r
Hugh Williams
Thom^s: Broocke

[26]   [1743 Processioning]
In obedience to an order of Vestry held for South Farnham parish ye 11th: day of July 1743. Wee the subscribers have procession^d ye lands as followeth beginning at ye lower end of the County ye 10th day of Novemb^r 1743.

Processioned ye line between Capt. William Mountague and Rice Jones, ye line between Wm: Buford & Wm Baskett, ye line between Wm Baskett & Francis Taylor, ye line between Capt Alexander Parker & John White, ye line between Capt Parker & Rebeckah Duckworth ye line between Rice Jones & Rebeckah Duckworth the line between Capt. Parker & Rice Jones Capt Mountague Charles Lee Thom^s: Buford Wm Buford Alexander Bomar being present.

Novemb^r: ye 11th 1743:
Processioned ye land between John White and Diana Stockley the line between John Massey & Thom^s: Clerk John Massey present the line between Wm: Richeson & Mary Shelton Anthony Ridgaway James Shelton present and ye line between Wm Richeson & John Massey ye line between Wm: Richeson & Charlott Mountague John Massey & John Madaris present ye line between John Massey & Capt Mountague ye line between John Massey & Dianna Stockley John Massey present

Novemb^r ye 19th
Processioned ye line Bewteen Capt Parker & Thom^s: Dean the line between Thom^s Dean & Charlott Mountague the line between John Bush & Charlote Mountague Thom^s Broocke & John Dean present.

Novemb^r y^e 22^d
Processioned y^e line between Capt Mountague & Charlott Mountague & y^e line between Thom^s: Paine & Charlote Mountague Thom^s Pain & Charlote Mountague Thoms Paine present.

Novemb^r: y^e 29th
Procession$^{?d}$ y^e line Between Capt Alexander Parker John Bush y^e line between Capt Parker & William Broocke & the line between Capt Parker & Dianna Stockley the line between Stockley & Broocks y^e line between Wm: Broocks & John Bush the line between John Bush & Thoms Dean Peter Broocks present.

Novemb^r ye 30th
Processioned the line between Capt Parker & Capt Mountague Thom^s: Broocks Peter Broocks John Croudas present.

Processioned ye line between Capt Joshua Frye Quarter Land & Thom^s Pain Thom^s: Broocks present and ye line between Thom^s Pain & Capt Mountague Thomas Pain & Jam^s Parrott being present.

         Rice Jones
         John his HH mark Bush

[27] [1743 Processioning]
Processioned ye land of John Hail & Richd Compton & Thoms Gatewood.
Processioned ye land of Jam^s: Allen Benjamin Hail and John Hail jun^r.
Processioned the land of John Allen Peter Kemp & Henry Hayes.
Processioned the land of George Reeves John Allen & Harbet Waggener.
Processioned ye land of Susanna Meader Wm Meader and Wm Meader & Thom^s: Bell.
Processioned the land of Zachary Allen Saml Wagginer & David Faulkner.
Processioned ye land of John Pettis & Thom^s Burnett and John Bennett.
Nathaneel Pendletons land not processioned no body was [there] to shew

y̆ˣ lines.
Joseph Wilson & Robert Colemans Lands not processioned no body to shew yᵉ lines.
Processioned yᵉ lands of Thomˢ Bush in our precinct.
Processiond yᵉ part of Jnᵒ Boughans in our precinct.
Given from under our hands this 29ᵗʰ of Decembʳ 1743.

       John Bennett
       Thomas Bush

In Pursuance of an order of Vestry of South Farnham Parish dated July yᵉ 11ᵗʰ: 1743 Wee the processioned the land as followeth Viz

January yᵉ 9ᵗʰ: 1743: Wee processioned yᵉ land of John Hill Robert Seayers & John Billups present

We processioned yᵉ land of Richᵈ Upshaw Robert Seayres & John Bellups present. We processioned yᵉ land of Daniel Sillavan Robert Seayers & John Billups present. Wee processioned yᵉ land Edward Webb Robert Seayres & John Billups present. We processioned yᵉ land of Daniel Sellivan Robert Seayers & John Billups present. Wee could not procession yᵉ land of Capᵗ Thomˢ: Sthreshley deceasᵈ being Orphans Land. We could not procession the land of Cap. Thoˢ Belfield decᵈ being orphans land.

Wee could not procession ye land of Robert Broocking he being not present. Wee could not procession yᵉ land of Capᵗ Francis Smith his overseer had no orders to shew yᵉ lands. Wee could not procession yᵉ lines between Mʳ. William Fantilleroy & Capᵗ. Francis Smith no body to shew the bounds for Smith. Wee processioned yᵉ line between William Fantilleroy & Thomˢ Wareing junʳ. Wee could not procession yᵉ land of Nicholas Layford he not being at home.

[28] [1743 Processioning]
Wee could not Procession yᵉ land of Abraham Padgett deceasᵈ: being orphans land. Wee could not procession yᵉ line between Thomˢ: Wareing junʳ: & Nicholas Layford he not at home. Wee processioned y Lifie between Thomˢ Wareing junʳ: and John Mearitt John Pagget present. Wee could not procession yᵉ lands between Robert Broocking & John Mearitt

Brooking not present. Wee could not procession ye land of Henry Tandy Deceas^d being Orphan's land.
Jany ye 25th 1743   John Seayres
                                 Thoms Wareing jun^r

Pursuant to an order of Vestry baring date ye 11th day of July 1743 Wee the Processioners have processioned all the lands in our precinct Viz^t

Processioned ye land of Benjamin Smith in the presence of Thomas Edmondson. Processioned ye lands of Capt Peacheys in presence of John Tyler W^m: Tyler Jam^s: Turner John Pagen. Processioned the land of John Tyler in ye presence of James Turner. Procession^d ye land of Mr Boog [?] in presence of Jam^s: Turner. Procession^d ye land of W^m: Tyler in presence of Jam^s: Turner. Processioned the land of Jam^s Turner in presence of Leonard Williamson & Thom^s: Williamson. Processioned ye land of George Turner in presence of James Turner. Processioned ye land of Jam^s: Fisher & Benjamin Fisher in presence of John Page Thom^s Williamson & Leonard Williamson. Processioned ye land of Thom^s: Williamson in presence of John Pain Leonard Williamson & Thom^s Williamson. Processioned ye land of John Williamson in presence of Thom^s Williamson & John Pane.

Processioned ye land of Elizabeth Cooper in presence of John Pane Thom^s: Williamson Leonard Williamson. Processioned ye land of Elizth Cooper jun^r: in presence of John Pane Thom^s Williamson Leonard Williamson. Processioned ye land of Jno Shurden in presence of John Pane Thom^s Williamson & Leonard Williamson. Processioned ye land of Edward Hays in presence of William Gorden John Williamson & Robert Acres.

Processioned ye land of John Williamson jun^r: in presence of Leonard Williamson. Processioned ye land of Mary Brisendine in presence of John Cox Thom^s: Cox and Jane Acres. Processioned ye land of Thom^s: Williamson Deceas^d in presence of John Cox & Thom^s Cox.

[29]   [1743 Processioning]
Processioned the land of Thom^s: Cox in presence of Jno: Cox.
Processioned the land John Cox in presence of Thom^s: Cox.

Processioned ye land of Richd Bresendine in presence of John Cox & Thom^s: Cox.
Processioned ye land of Jams: Boughan jun^r.
All the land in our precinct was peaceably processioned.
Witness our hands this 23^d day of Decemb^r 1743.
       Benjamin Fisher
       Jam^s Fisher
       Jam^s Boughan jun^r

In obedience to an order of Vestry of the parish of South Farnham in ye County of Essex made ye 11th day of July 1743 Wee the Subscribers on ye 3rd day of Decemb^r: 1743 processioned ye lands in ye s^d order mentioned as followeth Viz^t Beginning at William Cheneys Then Processioned ye line between ye s^d Cheney Daniell Dobyns Bibby Bush Thom^s: Blatt deceas^d present Dan^{ll} Dobyns & Richd Johnson; also ye land of John Bush Charles Breedlove Isaac Johnson & Elizabeth FitsJeffries & Thom^s: Cooper present ye Proprietors etc.

4th: also the land of Jno Cox & Thom^s: Cox present ye Proprietors & Edward Williamsons also ye land of Edward Williamson & William Williamson John Rodden & John Davis & William Gordon present ye Proprietors etc.

ye 10th also ye land of Richd Johnson Jno: Hoskins Jno: Tribble Catherine Dunkin & William Trebble present Charles Breedlove & ye Proprietors etc.

Jany ye 11th: also ye land of John Hardee present William Trebble also ye land of Micajah Evans & Willm Hathaway Thomas Kidd & Thom^s Edmondson present William Breedlove in behalf of Hathaway & the Proprietors also ye lands of Thom^s Williamson & William Fletcher & Benjamin Fisher present Thom^s: Edmondson & ye s^d Proprietors, also ye land of William Hames Mary Clerk & Jam^s: Byram present Proprietors.
       M. Evans
       B Bush
       John Hardee

In obedience to an order of Vestry of the parish of South Farnham in the

County of Essex made ye 11th day of July anno Dom: 1743 Wee the Subscribers on ye 22nd & 23rd of Decemb^r Last past processioned the Lands in s^d order returned as followeth Viz^t: Beginning at the Honable Mr Robinsons Quarter & then we processioned ye land of Thom^s: Johnson & William Mitchell present George Russell Philip Johnson Stephen Neal & ye proprietors also ye land formerly belonging to John Dyke present John Minter and John Dike also ye land of Jno Minter & John Cammell Deceasd the heirs at Law & Jno: Dike present, also the lines between Thomas Johnson and Isaac Mitchell present John Dikes & Jno: Minter & the s^d proprietors also ye line between Sam^ll Piles & Jno: Cammell.

[30] [1743 Processioning]
By consent of ye s^d Piles ye s^d Cammell being present.

March ye 31st: 1744 Also processioned ye Land of the s^d Piles and ye Land in occupation of Nathaneel Pendleton present ye s^d Piles also ye Line between ye land of the s^d Pendleton & John Evans jun^r present ye s^d Piles.

Given under our hands this 2^d day of April anno Dominy 1744.
     Jno Evans jun^r
     N Pendleton

Pursuant to an order of Vestry held the 11th: day of July 1743 wee the subscribers have quietly & peaceably processioned all the Lands in our precincts. Given under our hands Jany 15th 1743:
     Wm: Dunn
     John Edwards
     John Fergeson

According to our order Wee have processioned our Lines in our precinct beginning Novemb^r: ye 16th at Capt Frys Line & the Lines of Mrs Ann Smiths Charles Hodges and Charles Sanders with us, then M^rs: Mountagues James Medleys Jam^s: Parrott & John Smith with us.

17th: M^r: Vass & Capt Beals & M^r: Corbens & M^rs: Adams & Jacob Abbott & W^m: Jones with us.

20th Then the Gleab Line & M^r: Vass Line by the Gleab: the Rever^d Mr.

Philips & M^r: Vass W^m: Jones with us.

22^d: Jam^s: Medleys Line & M^r: Vass old plantation line Peter Broocke & James Medley with us.

23rd: Then our own Lines which is the last, Charles Hodges and John Ross[?] with us.

         Joshua Boughton
         John X Boughton

In obedience to an order of Vestry Dated ye 11th day of July 1743 Wee the subscribers procession^d ye Land as followeth

Decemb^r: ye 15th Then processioned ye Line between Henry Young & John Young in company of ye s^d Henry & John Young.
16th: Then Wee processioned the remainder of M^r: Henry Youngs Land in Company with Jno Lewis & Henry Young.
18th: A line between Capt Francis Smith & Richd Cauthorn in Company of M^r: Henry Young & ye s^d Smith & Richd Cauthorn & Vincent Cauthorn.

And all ye rest of ye Lands in our precinct included with Col^l John Robinsons Esqr land & he being sick & not able to shew us ye Lines who proceeded no further Given from under our hands etc.

         Richd Tyler
         Williamson Young

[31] [1743 Processioning]
Wee the subscribers appointed processioners began ye 12th of Decembr and processioned Richd Gatewoods Mary St John Thom^s: Howertons Thom^s: Howerton Jam^s: Howerton & Jno: Dunn in Company ye 13th: Procession'd Edward Hays & Mr: Herds and Thomas Colemans Francis Attwoods & Mr. Towns land. Thom^s: Coleman Jno: Dunn Jam^s Femester in Company.

The 19th Processioned Joseph Mans Lewis Watkins one Line of M^{rs}: Elizth Bohannah John Baker forbad processioning his land Wm: Crows unprocessioned by reason he never wou[l]d come to shew us ye line.

Jany ye 25th: Processioned Eliz^a: Bohannahs Wm: Langhams William Covingtons & Sam^ll Coats William Covington Samuell Coats William Langham in Company.

27th: Processioned Jam^s: Newbill George Newbills & Rhodes Greenwoods Thom^s: Howerton Geoffrey Purkins & Rodes Greenwood in Company.

30th: Processioned Griffin Purkins Eliz^a: Cole Richd Covington Eliz^a Shepherd Eliz^a Staint Dan^ll Dobyns Jeremiah Shepherd Greffin Purkins Richd Conington Dan^ll Dobyns in Company.

January ye 30th: 1743   Richd Gatewood
                                 Jam^s: Newbill
                                 Geo: Newbill

In obedience to an Order of Vestry bearing Date ye 11th day of July 1743: Wee the Processioners have Processioned all ye lands in our Precincts & Every mans Land was peaceably processioned in our Precincts. Witness our hands
                                 Thom^s: Dunn
                                 Peter Dickinson
                                 Richd Brown

According to an order of Vestry bareing date ye 30th day of July 1743 Wee have processioned all ye lands in our precincts as followeth:

The line between John Croxton & Timothy Discoll in the presence of James Croxton & John Croxton. The line between Timothy Discoll & Capt William Aylott in the presence of James Croxton Jn° Croxton & John Harper.

The line between Thom^s Miller & Timothy Discoll in ye presence of Jam^s Croxton John Croxton John Harper & Jam^s Younger. The line between Capt Wm Aylett & Thom^s Miller in the presence of Timothy Discoll.

[32]   [1743 Processioning]
The line between Capt W^m: Aylett & Richd Jones in the presence of Richd Hodges Jam^s: Croxton Jn° Croxton. The line between Richd Jones & Jonathan Clerk in the presence of Jam^s: Croxton Jn°: Croxton Richd

Hodges. The Line between Capt Wm Aylett & Jonathan Clerk in ye presence of Jam.^s^ Croxton & John Croxton & Richard Hodges. The line between George Right & Robert Mash in the presence of John Smith W.^m^: Cox jun.^r^

The line between John Pickett & Robert Mash in the presence of John Powell W.^m^: Cox & Henry Cox. The line Between John Pickett & W.^m^: Cox in the presence of Jno Powell Jno: Smith & W.^m^: Cox jun.^r^. The Line between Co.^ll^ George Braxton & John Pickett the s.^d^ Jno: Pickett stopt ye Processioners in the presence of John Powell Wm Cox jun.^r^ & Henry Cox. The Line between W.^m^: Cox & Co.^ll^ George Braxton the s.^d^ W.^m^: Cox would not agree to let ye line be processioned.

The Line Between George Right & Wm Cox in the presence of W.^m^: Cox jun.^r^ Henry Cox & John Pickett & Jam.^s^ Harrenton. The line between John Pickett & W.^m^: Cox in the presence of W.^m^: Cox Henry Cox Jam.^s^ Harrinton. The line between W.^m^: Cox & Samuell Allen in ye presence of W.^m^: Cox jun.^r^. The line between Samuell Allen & Thomas Harrerd in ye presence of W.^m^: Cox jun.^r^.

The line between Jno: Ball & M.^rs^: Mary Latane in the presence of Jno: Powell & Sam.^ll^: Allen. The line Between Jno: Ball & Joseph Reeves in the presence of Jno: Powell & Sam.^ll^: Allen. The Line between Robert Price & Joseph Reeves in the presence of Jno: Powell Samuell Allen & Jno: Ball. The line between Joseph Reeves & Co.^ll^ George Braxton in presence of John Ball Jno: Powell & Sam.^ll^: Allen.

The line between Co.^ll^ George Braxton & John Ball the Indian Grant Patten in the presence of Joseph Reeves Sam.^ll^: Allen Jno: Powell. The line between John Ball & John Lumpkin in the presence of Joseph Reeves Sam.^ll^: Allen Jno: Powell.

The line Between Co.^ll^ George Braxton & Jno: Ball the s.^d^ John Ball told the Processioners that they might goe on the Near line but he would not agree that it to be his line so wee did not proceed on it. The Line between George Right & Capt Wm Aylett in the presence of Richd Hodges Jno: Harper & George Right jun.^r^.

Given under our hands   Jam^s Boughan
John Croxton
George Wright

[33]   [1743 Processioning]
Pursuant to an order of Vestry of South Farnham parish Dated July ye 11th 1743 To whome the sd order were directed to wee proceed as follows: Vizt

Beginning Novemb^r: ye 26th: 1743 processioned all the Lands in our precinct except Capt William Dangerfields & Mr: Mann Pages the reason of our not processioning theirs was no person appear'd to shew us the lines. Given under our hands this 19th day of Decemb^r: 1743.
                         James Gatewood
                         Francis Attwood

Pursuant to an Order of Vestry made ye 11th of July 1743 Wee the Subscribers have processioned ye Lands as followeth

Novemb^r: ye 28th: Processioned between Jno. Gatewood Senr and Isaac Gatewood & Between Jno: Gatewood jun^r & Jno: Gatewood Senr Present Jno: Gatewood jun^r & Isaac Gatewood.

Decemb^r: ye 12th Processioned between Thoms Hale & James Gatewood & between Mary Dix & Thom^s: Hail & between Richd Comton & Thom^s Haile & between Thom^s Haile Benjamin Haile & between Richd Compton & Mary Dix & between Richd Compton & Thom^s: Gatewood and between Thom^s: Gatewood & William Dix & between John Hunt & Thom^s: Gatewood & between Thom^s Bell & Thom^s Gatewood & between William Dix & Jno Hunt & between Jno: Allen & Jno: Hunt & between Jno: Allen & George Moody & between Jno: Allen & Jane Gordon & Between William Dix & Jane Gordon present John Hunt Thoms: Hail George Moody Jno: Allen Thom^s: Gatewood.

Decemb^r: ye 17th: Processioned between George Coleman & Mary Dix & between Jam^s: Gatewood & Jno Allen and between Mary Hull & William Dix & between George Coleman & Mary Latane & between Mary Latane & Jane Gordon & between William Roan & Mary Latane & between

William Roan & Jane Gordon & between George Moody & Jane Gorden & between George Moody & John Hunt & between William Roan & Jeremiah Upshaw Present W^m: Dix Jno: Hunt John Allen George Moody Jno: Latane George Coleman.

Decemb^r: ye 29th Processioned between Jno: Gatewood & William Roan & between Nicholas Pamplin Jno Gatewood & between William Roan & Nicholas Pamplin & between Rod Gorden & Thom^s: Johnson & between William Roan & Thom^s: Johnson & between Wm Roan & Nicholas Pamplin & between Edward Davis & John Gatewood present Capt William Roan Philip Gatewood Robert Johnson Thom^s: Roan. The land of Gregory Smith & Robert Price not processioned for want of shewing the lines.

         John his I mark Gatewood
         Nicholas Pamplin

[34] [1743 Processioning]
Pursuant to an order of Vestry of South Farnham Parish dated the 11th day of July 1743 Wee the subscribers have processioned the lands in the Mill Neck as followeth.

Beginning at John Armstrongs Land Land wee processioned the line which divideth ye s^d Armstrongs land from John Bournes present William Dangerfield Isaac Scandrett John Armstrong John Bourne Ben Allen jun^r.

Then wee went along the line which divideth ye land of William Dangerfield from John Bournes Land in presence of the above mentioned persons & the line which divideth ye s^d Dangerfields Land from James & William Greenhills Land.

Then Wee went along ye line which divideth John Bournes Land from Capt Alexander Parkers Land in the presence of the persons above mentioned.

Then Wee went along ye line which divides ye Land of William Dangerfield from ye land of Capt Alexander Parkers land present Henry Reeves Isaac Scandrett William Dangerfield.

Then Wee went along the Line which divides William Dangerfields Land from ye Land of Henry Reeves as far as the miles and both parties agreed to refer the processioning of Lines lately in dispute for reason which concerns themselves present Henry Reeves, William Dangerfield, Isaac Scandrett.

Then Wee went along the line which divides ye Land of M^r: Isaac Scandrett from Capt Alexander Parkers Land in presence of s^d Scandrett William Dangerfield Henry Reeves.

Wee processioned the line which divides ye Land of William Dangerfield from ye land of Isaac Scandrett present Henry Reeves Isaac Scandrett William Dangerfield.

The other Lands in our precinct either belongeth to orphans or adjoyns to orphans Land which wee humbly conceive is not to be processioned during ye minority of the s^d orphans. Given under our hands this 11th day of January 1743/4.

> Ben Johnson
> Joseph Reeves jun^r
> Jam^s: Reeves

Pursuant to an order of Vestry held for South Farnham Parish ye 11th: day of July 1743: Wee the Subscribers have processioned the Severall persons Lands in our precinct as followeth (Vizt)

$Decemb^r$ y^e 10th 1743 Wee processiond a line between the Land of Man Page Esqr & John Chamberlain the same being shew'd us by y^e s^d Chamberlain & he only present. The Land of M^r: Patt Barcley not processioned because there was no one to shew us the bounds thereof.

[35]   [1743 Processioning]
Man Page Esqr y^e same
M^{rs}: Elizabeth Godfreys the Same
$Thom^s$: Gamess y^e same.

17th: Wee processioned a Line between Mr Gabriel Jones & William Smith present John Stone. Wee processioned the Land of M^{rs}: Sukey

Edmondson pres.^t Mr William Jones & Morris Knight. Wee processioned y.^e Land of M.^r: Gabriel Jones present M.^r: William Jones M.^r: Thom.^s: Edmondson jun.^r M.:^r John Edmondson & Morris Knight. Wee processioned the Land of Mr Jam.^s Jones present Mr Thomas Edmondson jun.^r M.^r: William Jones M.^r: Jn.° Edmondson & Morris Knight.

Decemb.^r: ye 17th: 1743 Wee processioned the Land of Mr Thom.^s Edmonson jun.^r present M.^r: William Jones M: John Edmondson & Morris Knight.

19th: Wee processioned a Line between Man Page Esqr & Mr Joseph Amiss present M.^r: William Jones. Some part of the Bounds of M.^r: William Smiths Land and M.^r: Joseph Amiss not processioned because there was no one to shew us the Same.

Given under our hands this 19th day of Decemb.^r 1743.

James Jones
Gabriel Jones

In obedience to an Order of Vestry held for South Farnham parish ye 11th: day of July 1743 Wee the Subscribers have processioned the following persons land Viz.^t:

The Land of John Armstrong peaceably processioned present Benjamin Allen.
The Land of William Greenhills orphans peaceably processioned.
The Land of James Greenhills orphans peaceably processioned.
The Land of Christopher Beverley peaceably processioned.
The Land of Garrett Fitsimmons peaceably procession.^d
The Land of Dan.^ll Dayley peaceably processioned.
The Lines of Thom.^s Davis joyning on Fitsimmons & Dayley peaceably processioned still present Benjamin Allen.
The Land of Thom.^s Evans peaceably processioned present John Seayrs.
The Land of John Seayrs & ye upper line of Thom.^s Davis not processioned they both agreed not to have it done.
The Land of Howel Jones not processioned he being out of the countrey.
The Land of Thoms Wareing jun.^r not processioned nor the upper line of Benjamin Wagginer being on the Said

[36]   [1743 Processioning]
Waring by reason the said Waring never appeard to shew his bounds all ye remainder of the sd Wagginer land peaceably processioned present Benjamin Allen and Thom^s Evans. Witness our hands this 30th day of January 1743.

Benjamin Wagginer
John Bourne

Pursuant to an order of Vestry for South Farnham parish ye 11th: day of July 1743 Wee ye Subscribers being appointed processioners of ye upper precincts of ye s^d parrish did proceed as followeth.

Beginning ye 12th day of Decemb^r: & being accompanied with William Waller & Forrest Upshaw did procession the line between William Waller & Richd Upshaw on ye 11th day of January began at Jam ^{s}Rennolds Corner & being accompanied with James Rennolds Daneill Suillivan William Waller & William Rennolds did procession ye line between ye s^d James Rennolds & Richd Upshaw and James Rennolds & John Hilland another line between ye s^d James Rennolds & Richd Upshaw & William Rennolds & Richd Upshaw & John Upshaw & Richd Upshaw & Hannah Upshaw & William Waller & William Waller & William Gatewood ye s^d Gatewood not present & Richd Upshaw & William Gatewood and Hannah Upshaw & Richd Upshaw & William Rennolds & Forrest Upshaw & Thom^s: Coleman & William Rennolds & John Smether & William Rennolds ye s^d Smether being present.

On ye 12th: day of January processioned ye line between Thom^s: Coleman & Jno Smether & ye s^d Coleman and John Watkins & ye s^d Watkins & Jno Smether & the s^d Daniel Suillivan & Smither & y s Suillivan ^{e}and^d Wattkins, & ye s^d Suillivan & Jam : Rennolds, & y Said Côleman & Forrest Upshaw, & ye s^d Coleman & William Gatewood & finished ye s^d Colemans land.

On ye 29th day of January Wm Waller absent Forrest Upshaw present did procession ye lines between y ^{e}s ^{d}Forrest Upshaw & W Gatewood present ye s^d William Gatewood & Isaac Gatewood & Hannah Upshaw & W^m: Rennolds, & Richd Upshaw & W^m: Rennolds, & ye Dividing line between ye s^d Jam^s Rennolds & Wm Rennolds & So concluded.

The Land of Richd Holt Absalom Wells & Howels orphans not processioned by reason no body to shew ye lines given under our hands this 26th day of January 1743.

         John Wattkins
         Thom^s Coleman
         Richd Upshaw

[37] [1743 Processioning]
Pursuant to an Order of Vestry dated 11th of July 1743 We the Subscribers have processioned the lines as follows: Viz

The line between Adams orphans and Pains Orphans not processioned the Heirs at Law being in their minority.
The line between Thomas Williams and Captn Bird processioned in presence of Thomas Williams.
The line between Thomas Williams and Joshua Boughton processioned in presence of Thomas Williams.
The line between Thomas Williams and Thomas Brook processioned in presence of Thomas Williams and Samuel Brook.
The line between Thomas Williams and Alexander Roane dec^d processioned in presence of Thos Williams and Samuel Brook.
The line between Wm Broock & John Broock processioned in prst of John Broock & Sam^{ll} Broock.
The line between Wm Broock & Sam^{ll} Broocke processioned in present of Sam^{ll} Broock & Thos. Williams.
The line between John Phillips & Thos. W^{ms} processioned in present of ye said parties.
The line between Thom^s. W^{ms} & Capt Peachey processioned in present of Thos. W^{ms} & Sam^{ll} Broock.
The line between Capt Bird & Pains orphans not processioned ye Heir at law being in his minority.
The line between Pains orphans & Smiths orphans not processioned ye heirs at law being in their minority.
The line between Capt. Bird & Smith processioned in present Wm Mountague.
The line between Joshua Bouten & Thos. Broocke processioned in present of ye said parties.

The line between Sam[ll] Broock & John Phillips processioned in present of the said parties.
The line between John Phillips & John Evans j[r] processioned in present of the said parties.
The line between John Smith & John Broock processioned in present of the said parties.
The between John Smith & Sam[ll] Broock processioned in present of the said parties.
The line between John Smith & John Evans jun[r] processioned in present of John Broock & John Smith.
The line between John Evans j[r] & Margaret Bushnell processioned in present George Russell.
The line between Margaret Bushnells & Mitchells orphans not processioned the Heir at law being in his minority.
The line between W[m]son Young & Mitchells orphans not processioned the Heir at [law] being in his minority.
The line between John Evans and John Dunn processioned in present of Greensbe Evans.
The line between John Dunn & John Evans j[r] not processioned no body to shoe the line.
The line between John Evans & John Evans jun[r] processioned in present of Greensbe Evans.
The line between John Evans & W[m]son Young processioned in present of Greensbe Evans.
The line between W[m]son Young & Mitchells orphans not processioned the Heir at law being in his minority.

[38]   [1743 Processioning]
The line between Cap[t] Sam[ll] Peachey & John Philips possessioned in the prsents of the sd Parties.
The line Between Henry Young & John Young processioned in present of s[d] Parties.
The Line Between John Young & John Webb processioned in present of the said parties.
The Line Between Williamson Young & the Honoble John Robinson Esquire not processioned, no body to shew the Line.
The Line Between the Hon'oble John Robinson Esq[re] & John Young Processioned, present John Allen.

The Line Between John Webb & the orphans of sd Hill dec^d orphans not processioned the heir at Law being in his minority.
The Line Between Hills orphans & John Evans not processioned the heir at law being in his minority.
The Line Between John Evans j^r & Hills orphans not processioned the heir at Law being in his minority.
The Line Between Capt. Sam^{ll} Peachey & Hills orphans not processioned the heir at Law being in his minority.

        John Webb
        John Young
        John Phillips

Truly Registered p^r Jno Vass Clk to ye Vestry
   Examined p^r Fr^s Smith &
           W Roane   Church Wardens

****

[39]   [1747 Processioning]
Pursuant to an order of Court to ye County of Essex bareing date ye twenty first day of July anno Dominey one thousand seven hundred forty & seven whereby it is ordered that the Vestry of each parrish within ye s^d County divide their parishes into so many precincts as to them shall seem most convenient for processioning every particular persons land in the several parishes & appoint ye particular lines for processioning likewise appoint two intelligent honest freeholders at least of every precinct to see such processioning perform'd & take & return to ye Vestry an acct of every persons Lands they shall procession and of ye persons present at ye same & what Lands within precincts they shall fail to procession & of ye particular reasons of such failure.

This present Vestry do therefore divide ye parish of South Farnham into Twenty precincts and it is ordered that M^r: Rice Jones John Bush & Thoms Dunn or any two of them procession Every persons Lands in their precinct beginning at ye lower end of Essex County and run to the Gleab Creek from thence to M^r. Leonard Hills Quarter on ye Dragon and make their return as the Law directs beginning ye tenth day of Novemb^r

& to finish by ye last of ye same month & to make their return as the Law directs.

Ordered that Joshua Boughton John Boughton & Jam^s Medley or any two of them procession Every person Land in their precinct beginning at M^r: Leonard Hills Quarter on ye Dragon from thence to Joshua Boughton & so to ye Dragon & from thence to Mrs Adams Quarter on ye river side beginning ye fifteenth day of Novemb^r & to finish by ye last of ye same month & to make their return as the Law directs.

Ordered that Nicholas Smith jun^r: Sam^ll: Smith & William Broocke or any two of them procession Every person Lands in their precinct beginning at Joshua Boughtons from thence up to John Dickes from thence to William Cheney on ye Dragon beginning ye twentieth day of Novemb^r & to finish by ye twentieth day of Decemb^r & to make their return as ye Law directs.

Ordered that John Dunn John Young & John Philips or any two of them procession Every persons Lands in their precinct beginning at M^rs. Adams Quarter on ye River Side from thence to Capt Tylers Creek by John Youngs & so to ye Back Road by Thomas Cauthorns from thence down ye s^d road to Joshua Boughton beginning ye twenty second day of Novemb^r & to finish by ye thirty second day of Decemb^r & to make their return as ye Law directs.

Ordered that John Evans jun^r Ludy Piles & John Minter or any two of them procession Every persons lands in their precinct beginning at Col^l Robinsons Quarter land by Thom^s Cauthrons from thence to John Dickes from thence down ye Mill Swamp to Piscatua Ferry so down ye Main Road to Col^l Robinsons Quarter old field beginning y twenty sixth day of Novemb^r & to finish by ye twenty sixth day of Decemb^r & to make their return as the law directs.

[40]   [1747 Processioning]
Ordered that Capt Richd Tyler William Lowry and Jam^s Webb or any two of them procession Every persons lands in their precinct beginning at Col^l Robinsons Quarter Land by Thom^s Cauthorn from thence to ye Creek where John Philips once lived & all ye land between ye River & y^e

Road to Piscatua Creek beginning ye twenty eighth day of Novemb^r & to finish by ye first day of January & to make their return as ye Law directs.

Ordered that Micajah Evans Bibby Bush & John Vass jun^r or any two of them procession Every person lands in their precinct beginning at William Cheneys on ye Dragon from thence to ye land of Covingtons Mill Swamp & down ye Swamp to Coll Tylers Quarter Landing from thence up ye Road by Thom^s Williamson to William Cheneys beginning ye third day of Decemb^r: and to finish by ye twelfth day of January & to make their return as the Law directs.

Ordered that James Boughan jun^r: Benjamin Smith & Thomas Williamson or any two of them procession Every person Land in their precinct beginning at Coll Smiths Quarter Landing & so up Piscatua Creek to ye old mill from thence along ye Road to Harpers Ordinary from thence down ye branch to ye Dragon & to William Cheney from thence to Coll Tylors Quarter r beginning ye fifth day of Decemb^r & to finish by ye fifteenth day of January & to make their return as the Law directs.

Ordered that Thomas Dunn Peter Dickason & Richd Brown or any two of them procession Every persons land in their precinct beginning at Matthews bridge from thence to ye Road & down ye Road to Elliotts old field from thence to ye head of ye Dragon and down ye Dragon to a branch below Jam^s: Finnys from thence up ye s^d branch to Harpers Ordinary & so along ye Road to Matthews bridge beginning ye tenth day of Decemb^r & to finish by ye last day of January & to make their return as ye Law directs.

Ordered that Richd Gatewood George Newbill & Richd Covington or any two of them procession Every persons Land in their precinct beginning between ye two branches of ye Dragon from thence up to ye Main Road that divideth Essex County from King & Queen County beginning ye twelfth day of Decemb^r & to finish by ye last day of January & to make their return as ye Law directs.

Ordered that William Dunn John Edmondson & Benjamin Johnson or any two of them procession Every persons Land in their precinct beginning at Hales bridge from thence down ye Road to ye long branch head from thence to ye head of Fishers mill Swamp & down ye Swamp to Matthews bridge from thence along ye Road to ye old mill from thence up ye Swamp to Hails bridge beginning ye tenth day of Novemb^r & to finish by ye last day of ye same month & to make their return as ye Law directs.

Ordered that Thomas Brasher Sam^{ll} Allen & George Wright or any two of them procession Every person land in their precinct beginning at Hails bridge from thence to ye long reach road from thence up ye road to ye dividing line of ye County from thence by ye head of Piscatua Swamp & so down ye Swamp to Hails bridge beginning ye fifteenth day of Novemb^r & to finish by ye last of ye same month & to make their return as ye Law directs.

[41]   [1747 Processioning]
Ordered that Jam^s Jones John Chamberlain & Thom^s Games or any two of them procession every persons lands in their precinct beginning at Hardees Ferry on Hoskins Creek from thence to Piscatua Ferry & so down each creek to ye River beginning ye twentieth day of Novemb^r & to finish by the twentieth day of Decemb^r & to make their return as the law directs.

Ordered that James Gatewood Joseph Burnett & Thomas Bush or any two of them procession Every person Lands in their precincts between ye Little Ferry on Hoskins Creek & Piscatua Ferry & up to Boughan Mill & so up to Whites Run Bridge beginning ye twenty second day of Novemb^r & to finish by ye twenty second day of Decemb^r & to make their return as the law directs.

Ordered that Henry Harper John Hail & Sam^{ll} Allen or any two of them procession Every persons land in their precinct between Boughans Mill & so across to Warings Mill and so up to Hails bridge & so across to Warings Mill Swamp beginning ye twenty sixth of Novemb^r & to finish by ye twenty fourth of Decemb^r & to make their return as ye law directs.

Ordered that Joseph Reeves George Moody John Hunt & John Gatewood or any of them procession Every persons land in their precinct between Hails bridge & Warings Mill Swamp up to ye dividing line of Essex County from King & Queen County: beginning ye twe[n]ty eighth day of Novemb[r] & to finish by y[e] first day of January & to make their return as y[e] Law directs.

Ordered that Maj[r]: William Dangerfield Isaac Scandrett & Robert Coleman or any two of them procession Every persons Land in y[e] Mill Neck from John Armstrong & so across to William Greenhills beginning y[e] third day of Decemb[r] & to finish by y[e] twelfth day of January & to make their return as y[e] law directs.

Ordered that Benjamin Wagginer John Allin jun[r] & John Bourn or any two of them procession Every persons land in their precinct between John Armstrong & William Greenhills & Major Warings Mill & so across to Henry Tandys beginning y[e] fifth day of Decemb[r] and to finish by y[e] fifteenth day of January & to make their return as y[e] Law directs.

Ordered that John Sears Thom[s] Waring jun[r] & Francis Jones or any two of them procession Every persons Lands in their precinct between Major Warings Mill & Henry Tandy & so up to Charles Wallers from thence to Mr Jam[s] Rennolds beginning y[e] tenth day of Decemb[r] & to finish by y[e] last day of January & to make their return as y[e] Law directs.

Ordered that Richd Upshaw Forrest Upshaw & Thomas Coleman or any two of them procession Every persons land in their precinct in the upper precinct to King & Queen beginning the twelfth day of Decemb[r] & to finish by the last day of January & to make their return as the law directs.

                    Signed
                    Wm Stuart
                    Alexander Parker }
                    John Vass   } Church Wardens

Truly Registered p[r] Jn[o] Vass Clk of y[e] Vestry

****

[42]   [1751 Processioning]
Pursuant to an order of Court for the County of Essex baring date ye sixteenth day of July Anno Dominy one thousand seven hundred fifty &

one whereby is it ordered that the Vestry of each parish within ye s^d county divide their parishes into so many precincts as to them shall seem most convenient for processioning every particular persons lands in the several parishes and appoint the particular times for processioning, likewise appoint two intelligent honest freeholders at least of every precinct to see such processioning perform'd and take and return to ye Vestry an acc^t of every persons land they shall procession and of ye persons present at ye same & what lands in their precincts they shall fail to procession and of ye particular reasons of such failure.

This present Vestry do therefore divide ye parish of South Farnham into twenty precincts & it is ordered that M^r: Rice Jones John Wiley & Thoms Dean or any two of them procession Every persons lands in their precinct beginning at the lower end of Essex County & run to ye Gleab Creek from thence to M^r: Learn Hills Quarter on the Dragon & make their return as ye Law directs beginning ye tenth day of Novemb^r & to finish by ye last of ye same month & to make their return as the Law directs.

Ordered that John Boughton John Smith & Joseph Sanders or any of them procession every persons Lands in their precinct beginning at Mr Leonard Hills Quarter on ye Dragon from thence to Joshua Boughtons & so to ye Dragon & from thence to Mrs Adams Quarter on ye River Side beginning ye fifteenth day of Novemb^r & to finish by he last of ye same month & to make their return as the Law directs.

Ordered that Nicholas Smith jun^r: Sam^ll: Smith & William Broocke or any two of them procession Every persons Lands in their precinct beginning at Joshua Boughton from thence up to John Dikes from thence up to William Cheneys on ye Dragon beginning ye twentieth day of Novemb^r & to finish by ye twentieth day of Decemb^r & to make their return as the Law directs.

Ordered that John Dunn John Philips & John Evans jun^r or any two of them procession Every persons Lands in their precinct beginning at M^rs: Adams Quarter on the River Side from thence to Capt Tylers Creek by John Youngs & so to ye Back Road by Thom^s: Cauthorns from thence down ye said Road to Joshua Boughtons beginning ye twenty second day of Novemb^r to finish by ye twenty second day of Decemb^r & to make their return as the Law directs.

Ordered that M^r: James Jones Ludy Piles & John Minter or any two of them procession Every persons Lands in their precinct beginning at Co^{ll} Robinsons Quarter land by Thom^s: Cauthorn from thence to John Dikes & from thence down ye Mill Swamp to Piscatua Ferry so down ye Main Road to Co^{ll} Robinsons Quarter old field beginning ye twenty sixth day of Novemb^r & to finish by ye twenty sixth day of Decemb 'and to make their return as ye Law directs.

Ordered that Capt Richd Tyler John Lowry & Vincent Cauthorn or any two of them procession Every persons Lands in their precincts beginning at Co^{ll} Robinsons Quarter Land by Thom^s Cauthorns from thence to ye Creek where John Phillips once lived & all the Land between ye River & ye Road to Piscatua Creek beginning ye twenty eighth day of Novemb^r & to finish by ye first day of January & to make their return as the Law directs.

Ordered that Micajah Evans John Vass jun^r & Thoms: Cox or any two of them procession Every persons Lands in their precinct beginning at William Cheneys on ye Dragon from thence to the head of Covingtons Mill Swamp & down the Swamp to Co^{ll} Tylers Quarter Landing from thence up the Road by Thom^s Williamson to William Cheneys beginning the third day of Decemb^r: & to finish by ye twelfth day of January & to make their return as the Law directs.

Ordered that Capt Benjamin Smith James Boughan jun^r: & Thom^s Williamson or any two of them procession Every persons Lands in their precinct beginning at Capt Benjamin Smiths Landing & so up Piscatua Creek to the old Mill from thence along ye Road to Edward Mays ordinary from thence down ye branch to ye Dragon & to William Cheneys from thence to Capt Benjamin Smiths Landing beginning ye fifth day of Dememb^r & to finish by ye fifteenth day of January & make their return as the Law directs.

[43] [1751 Processioning]
Ordered that Thomas Dunn Richard Brown & William Crow or any two of them procession every persons lands in their precinct beginning at Mathews Bridge from thence to the Road & down the Road to Elliotts

old field from thence to ye head of the Dragon & down ye Dragon to a branch below Jam^s Finnys from thence up ye said branch to Hayes Ordinary and so along the Road to Mathews Bridge beginning the tenth day of Decemb^r and to finish by the last day of January and to make their return as the Law directs.

Ordered that Richard Gatewood John Townley & Jams Coffland or any two of them procession every persons lands in their precinct beginning between ye two branches of ye Dragon from thence up to ye Main Road that divideth Essex County from King & Queen County beginning ye twelfth day of Decemb^r & to finish by ye last day of January & to make their return as the Law directs.

Ordered that John Edmondson Jams Banks & Ambrose Jones or any two of them procession Every persons Lands in their precinct beginning at Hales Bridge from thence down ye Road to ye Long Reach Road from thence to ye head of Fishers Mill Swamp & down the Swamp to Matthews Bridge from thence along ye Road to the old Mill from thence up ye Swamp to Hales Bridge beginning ye tenth day of Novemb^r & to finish by ye last day of ye same month & to make their return as the Law directs.

Ordered that Thom^s: Barker Sam^ll: Allin & William Cox jun^r: or any two of them procession Every persons Lands in their precinct beginning at Hales Bridge from thence to ye Long Reach Road from thence up ye Road to ye dividing line of ye County from thence to ye head of Piscatua Swamp & so down ye Swamp to Hales Bridge beginning fifteenth day of Novemb^r & to finish by the last of the same month.

Ordered that Thomas Wyatt John Chamberlain & Thomas Games or any two of them processioned Every persons lands in their precinct beginning at Hardees Ferry on Hoskins Creek from thence to Piscatua Ferry & so down each creek to ye River beginning ye twentieth day of Novemb^r & to finish by the twentieth day of Decemb^r & to make their return as the Law directs.

Ordered that Jam^s: Gatewood Joseph Russell & Thom^s: Bush or any two of them procession Every persons lands in their precinct [beginning at] ye Little Ferry on Hoskins Creek & Piscatua Ferry & up to Boughans Mill & so up to Whites Run Bridge beginning ye twenty second day of

Novemb^r & to finish by ye twenty second day of Decemb^r: & to make their returns as ye Law directs.

Ordered that Henry Harper John Haile & Jam^s: Allin or any two of them procession Every persons lands in their precinct Between Boughans Mill & so across to Warings Mill & so up to Hails Bridge & so across to Warings Mill Swamp beginning ye twenty sixth day of Novemb^r & to finish by ye twenty fourth day of Decemb^r & to make their return as ye Law directs.

Ordered that Forest Upshaw John Latane & George Coleman or any two of them procession Every persons Lands in their precinct between Hails Bridge & Warings Mill Swamp up to ye dividing line of Essex County from King & Queen County beginning ye twenty eighth day of Novemb^r & to finish by ye first day of January & to make their return as the law directs.

Ordered that Maj^r: William Dangerfield M^r: Isaac Scandrett & Jam^s: Reeves or any two of them procession Every persons Lands in the Mill [Neck] from John Armstrong & so across to William Greenhills beginning ye third day of Decemb^r & to finish by ye twelfth day of January & to make their return as the Law directs.

Ordered that William Edmondson Benjamin Allen & Dan^{ll} Dobyn or any two of them procession Every person Lands in their precincts between John Armstrong & William Greenhill & Col^l Warings Mill & so across to Henry Tandys beginning ye fifth day of Decemb^r & to finish by ye twelfth day of January & to make their return as ye Law directs.

Ordered that Thom^s Waring jun^r John Rennolds & Silvanus Tandy or any two of them procession Every persons lands in their precinct between Col^l Warings Mill & Henry Tandy & so up to Charles Wallers from thence to M^r: Jams Rennolds beginning ye tenth day of Decemb^r & to finish by ye last day of January & to make their return as ye law directs.

[44]   [1751 Processioning]
Ordered that William Gatewood Leonard Hill & John Swilby or any two

of them procession every persons land in their precinct in the upper precinct to King & Queen beginning the twelfth day of Decembr & to finish by the last day of January & to make their return as the law directs.

Sign^d
Alexander Cruden
John Vass   } Church Wardens:
John Clements

Truly Registered p^r John Vass Clk of ye Vestry

****

At a Vestry held for the parish of South Farnham at Capt: Jam^s: Jones Piscatua Ferry Aprill ye 10th 1752

    Present
    The Rever^d: Alexander Cruden
    M^r: John Vass   } Church Wardens
    M^r: John Clements

Capt: William Roan, Major William Dangerfield M^r: Jams Webb M^r: Thom^s: Waring M^r: John Upshaw

Ordered that the returns made by ye Processioners be truly registered in the Vestry Book & to be Examin'd over by ye Vestry to see that they be rightly Entr^d within six months after ye date hereof.

In obedience to an order of ye Gentlemen of ye Vestry of South Farnham parish baring date ye 27th: day of August 1751 We ye Subscribers have procession^d all ye Lands in ye precincts mentioned in ye said order.

Beginning Novemb^r: ye 15th: Procession^d y^ line Between M: Leonard Hill and Joseph Sanders; between Joseph Sanders & Jam^s: Medley Junr Robert Hunley & Joseph Sanders present. Processioned ye Line between ye Orphants of Abraham Mountague & Jam^s: Medley Junr: Between Jam^s Medley & M^r: Leonard Hill; Between Jam^s: Medley Junr & Capt William Beale Jam^s: Medley jun^r Joseph Sanders & Robert Hunley present.

Novemb.r 25th: Processioned ye Line Between ye Orphants of Abraham Mountague Deceasd & Jams: Medly junr Between Jams Medley jun: and Capt William Beale; Jams: Medley jun: Joseph Sanders & Jams: Gardner present.

Novembr: ye 26th: Processioned the Line Between Capt William Beale & Mr: John Vass Sen Between M: John Vass & M : Tabitha Adams Between Mr: John Vass & the Orphants of Abraham Mountague Deceasd Between Mr: John Vass & ye Gleab Land of South Farnham parish Between Capt William Beale & Richard Corbin Esqu 'Jacob Abbott & Jams Gardner present.

Novembr: ye 27th: Wee ye Subscribers processiond ye Line Between Richd Corben Esqur and Mrs. Tabitha Adams John Patterson present.

Decembr: ye 3d: Wee the Subscribers Procession dy eLine Between Capt William Beale & Jno Medley Senr Between Jams: Medley Senr & Ann Sanders Between Jams Medley Senr & Vincent Vass Between Vincent Vass and Capt William Beale Jam :sMedley Vincent Vass & Reuben Vass present Procession'd the Line between Vincent Vass & John Boughan Vincent Vass & Reuben Vass present.

Decembr: ye 4th: Processioned yf Line Between yf Land of John Boughton & ye land calld Mrs. Hannah Birds, the Line between Joshua Boughton & John Boughton William Boughton present Processiond the Line between Mr: John Armested & Joshua Boughton Between Mr: John Armisted & John Boughton Between Mr: John Armisted Joseph Patterson. Between Joseph Patterson & John Smith. Between John Armisted and John Smith. Between Joseph Patterson & John Boughton, William Boughton and John Boughton junr present. Given under our hands 11th day of January 1752.

        John Boughton
        John Smith

[45] [1751 Processioning]
In obedience to an Order of Vestry dated ye 27th of August 1751 Wee the Subscribers have processiond ye Lines as followeth

Beginning at ye Lower end of Essex County ye 11th: day of Novembr 1751 at a line Between Capt William Mountague & Rice Jones Capt Mountague & William Jones present.

Novemb^r: ye 15th: Procession^d ye line Between John Massey & John Wiley Between John Massey and Lewis Mountague ye line Between John Massey & Thom^s: Salt. Between Thomas Clerk & Jam^s Richeson Between John Massey and Thom^s: Clerk Between James Richeson & Abraham Mountagues Orphans Between Capt Mountague & John Massey, John Massey William Broocke Robert Clerk Thomas Clerk & Peter Richeson present.

Novemb^r: ye 16: Processioned ye line Between Capt Mountague and John Bush between Capt Mountague & Thom^s: Pain & Between Leonard Hill & Thomas Pain Between Thomas Pain & Abraham Mountagues Orphants Between Thomas Dean & John Bush Thoms: Dean & John Bush present.

Novemb^r: ye 17th: Procession^d ye Line between M^{rs}: Parker & John Bush Between M^{rs}: Parker & John Clerk Between M^{rs}: Parker & John Wiley between John Clark & John Bush Charles Lee John Bush Thoms Taff & Joseph Jones present.

March ye 23 The Line between M^{rs}: Parker & Augustine Owen between M^r: Rice Jones & John Cloudas Augustine Owen Thomas Taff Charles Lee John Cloudas & Josep[h] Jones present. The upper Line Between John Cloudas & M^{rs}: Parker one corner Tree not to be found & very few line Trees. M^{rs}: Parker not being present wee omitted processioning of it. Processioned ye Line between M^r: Rice Jones & M^{rs}: Parker Between M^{rs}: Parker & Capt William Mountague Charles Lee & Joseph Jones present the Line Between Jno: Wiley & John Bush John Bush & John Bush jun^r & Benjamin Dean present.

John Wiley
Thom^s his mark Dean

In obedience to an order of Vestry Wee ye Subscribers have mett & Procession^{ed} ye Line as followeth:

Novemb^r: ye 20th 1751 Procession^d ye Line Between Joshua Boughton & Vincent Hudson between Nicholas Smith & Andrew Hipkins between Nicholas Smith & Sam^{ll}: Broocke Between Nicholas Smith & John Broocke Between Major Francis Smith and John Broocke Between John Broocke & John Smith in the presence of John Boughton & John Broocke.

Novembr: ye 22nd Processioned the Line Between John Evans & Jno. Cheney in presence of John Evans & Peter Broocke.

Novemb^r: ye 27th Processioned ye line between John Cheney & John Lacey Between John Cheney & Richd Johnson Between John Cheney and Nicholas Smith jun^r: between Nicholas Smith jun^r and Richd Johnson between Nicholas Smith jun^r: & Abner Dobyns between Nicholas Smith jun^r & Edward Bomer in the presence of Isaac Broocke and Abraham St John.

Novemb^r ye 28th: Processioned ye line between Edward Bomer and Abner Dobyns between Edward Bomer & Bowler Dobyns between Edward Bomer & Thom^s Broocke & Francis Brisondine between Edward Bomer & Thomas Hasty in presence of Thomas Broocke & Edward Bomer.

Decemb^r ye 12th: Processioned the line between Thom^s Hasty & Jeremiah Shepherd between Jeremiah Shepherd & Thomas Newbill between Thomas Newbill & Henry Crutcher between Henry Cructher & William Broocke in presence of Thomas Newbill & Abraham St John.

[46]   [1751 Processioning]
Decemb^r ye 18th: Processioned ye line between Jeremiah Shepherd & Thom^s Broocke between Henry Crutcher & Andrew Hipkins in ye presence of Thoms Crutcher.

Decemb^r ye 19 Processioned ye Line between Major Francis Smith & Andrew Hipkins between Maj^r: Smith & Henry Crutcher between Major Francis Smith & Andrew Hipkins between Maj^r: Smith & Thomas Hasty between Major Smith & John Smith in ye presence of Philip Patterson.

Procession^d ye Line between William Broocke & Andrew Hipkins in the presence of Thom^s Newbill.

        Nicholas Smith jun^r
        Samuel Smith
        William Broocke

Pursuant to an order of Vestry held for South Farnham parish bearing date ye 27th day of August 1751 Wee ye Subscribers on ye 26th of Novemb^r in ye year above and began & Processioned y ^e Land of M :^r Peachey present ye Said Peachey & his Brother & on ye 27th day of ye s^d Novemb^r processioned the Land of M^rs: Adams & the Land of Joshua Boughton William Eals Isaac Williams & Vincent Hudsons to ye Main Road & also ye lines between ye s^d William[s] & Hipkins present John Jeffries & ye Boughtons & William Eals & Reuben Williams also ye Lands of John Broocke & Samll Broocke & Jno: Smith Procession^d ye Land of John Evans & John Dunns that is to say ye lines between their said Lands present Greensbee Evans also proceeded to procession the Land of M^r: John Webb and the above s^d John Evans & ye weather ye s^d day being very bad & a small dispute in a line between them which they both agreed to settle themselves some other day for which reasons wee did not procession their Lands & all other the Lands within ye precinct mentioned in ye s^d order belonging to infants or other persons in their minority. Given under our hands ye 17th day of Decemb^r 1751.

        John Dunn
        John Evans Junr

Pursuant to an order of Vestry held for the parish of South Farnham ye 27th day August Wee y ^e Subscribers have procession^d y ^e Lands in our precincts as followeth

Decemb^r ye 4th 1751 In presence of Thomas Johnson William Mitchell & John Dicke was processioned ye Land of Elizabeth Johnson & ye bounds of so much of ye Land of Doct^r: Philip Jones as is in our precinct & a line between Henry Faulkner & William Mitchell also a Line between William Mitchell and Thomas Johnson & John Cauthorn (an Infant) & a line between Thomas Johnson & Isaac Mitchells Orphans Lands so likewise a line between Isaac Mitchells Orphans Lands & ye Land of John Minter and a Line between Frances Minters Land and ye Land of Richard Jeffries.

5th: The lines between Richd Jeffries John Minter & Samuell Piles in presence of the Proprietors of their respective Lands.

12th: A Line Between Mr: Jams Jones & Ludo Piles in presence of John Mountague. Given under our hands this 12th day of Decembr 1751.

       James Jones
       Ludo Piles
       John Minter

In obedience to an order of Vestry dated ye 27th day of August last appointing us Processioners of Every persons Lands in our precinct & Wee accordingly met on ye 28th day of November following as in ye said order we were directed & processioned ye dividing line between ye Lands of John Robinson Esqr & ye orphans of Henry Young Gent deceaed in Company with Mr: John Tyler & Francis Jones.

And at another time wee met & processioned ye dividing line of the Lands of Majr: Francis Smith & Jams: Cauthorn each party being present also the dividing line between ye Lands of ye sd Smith & John Webb each party being also present also wee met at another time & processiond part of the dividing line of ye Lands of ye sd Smiths & Mr John Lowry Each party being present also in the presence of ye Reverd Alexandr: Cruden & Mr: Benjamin Rust.

[47] [1751 Processioning]
The weather proving so bad the other lands interperzing with orphans and no person appearing to shew us their lines prevented us from proceeding any further. Given under our hands this thirty first day Decembr anno dom 1751.

       Richd Tyler
       John Loury
       Vincent Cauthorn

In obedience to an order of Vestry made ye 27th: day of August 1751 Processioners have processioned Every persons Land to us mentioned Beginning at William Cheneys Deceasd on ye Dragon from thence to ye head of Mr: Covingtons Mill Swamp Including Every persons Lands in the said Precinct by ye s^d order mentioned. Given under our hands this 14th day of April 1752.

       Micajah Evans
       Thomas Cox
       John Vass jun^r

In obedience to an order of Vestry held for the parish of South Farnham ye 27th: of August 1751 for appointing Processioners Wee the Subscribers have accordingly processioned all the Land mentioned in the said order and have met with no obstructions except between M^r: Jam^s: McCaul & M^r: John Tyler where there was no line to be found.

       Thom^s: Williamson
       Jam^s: Boughan

According to an order wee the Subscribers have processioned all the land in our precinct Quietly & Peaceably.

       Thom^s Dunn
       Richd Brown

In obedience to any order of Vestry bareing date August ye 27th 1751 Wee being appointed Procession[ers] have processionrd ye Lands in our precinct as (Vizt) February ye 13th: processioned John Townleys John Deshazoes and William Deshazoes Land John Townley John Deshazo & William DeShazo present.

February ye 14th Processioned part of Joseph Mans Land part of Lewis Wattkins part of John Crows but could not procession all their Lands for want of Henry Baker that joyned to them, then processiond Jonathan Dunns Thom^s Hill John Langham Jonathan Dunn Thomas Hill John Langham present.

February ye 21st Processioned Capt William Covingtons George Newbills William Greenwoods Lands & Rhodes Greenwoods also Jam^s Newbill George Newbill James Carflaphere[?] present at ye time; then processionrd part of Sam^{ll}: Coats part of Jam^s: Newbills & part of John Harpers part of Thomas Howertons part of Jam^s Coughlands but could not procession all their Lands for want of M^r: John Armstead that Joynes to them.

February ye 24th Processioned Lucy Purkins Elizabeth Coats Thomas Henry Broocks Richd Covingtons Jeremiah Shepherds Richd Gatewoods John Howertons Obediah Howertons Richard Covington William Coale Thoms Henry Broocks present at ye time.

Henry Boughan refus'd to go & procession his land his reasons for it wee know not. Witness our hands this 25th day of February 1752.
       Richd Gatewood
       John Townley
       James Coughland

[48] [1751 Processioning]
In obedience to an order of Vestry held for the parish of South Farnham on August ye 27th 1751. Wee the Subscribers being appointed to procession the several persons lands in the said preceincts do make our return as follows.

Novembr: ye 27th: The land of Joseph Reeves peaceably processioned in ye presence of James Dix & Henry Stuart. The Land of John Ball not procession'd he being sick there being no person to shew his lines. The Land of George Braxtons orphans the same. The Land of Thomas Harrards orphans the same.

28th: The Land of George Wright peaceably procession'd Henry Cox present.
The Land of William Cox ye same George Wright Henry Cox present.
The Land of Samuell Allen ye same George Wright Henry Cox present.
The Land of Joseph Ryland not procession'd there being no person to attend to shew ye Lines.
The Land of John Pickett ye same.
The Land of Richd Jones peaceably procession'd Richd Hodges & Benjamin Jones present.
The Land called Ayletts Quarter Land ye same Richd Hodges present.

29th: The Land of William Fretwell peaceably procession'd Richd Hodges present.
The Line Between William Fretwell & James Booker ye same.

The Line Between Thoms Miller & Ayletts Quarter the same.
The Land of Thom^s: Barker the same. Jam^s Akres & Jam^s Mason present.
Given under our hand this 30th: day of Novemb^r 1751.

       Thom^s Barker
       Sam^{ll} Allen

Pursuant to an order of Vestry dated ye 27th day of August 1751 Wee the Subscribers to whome ye said order was directed to procession has proceeded as follows:
William Gatewoods Land processioned.
Wartuse Dunn Land processioned.
James Gatewoods Land processioned.
John Singletons Land processioned.
Thomas Bushs Land processioned.
John Boughan Land processioned.
John Greggs Land processioned.
Henry Purkins Land processioned.
Joseph Burnett Land processioned.
Capt Jam^s: Jones Land processioned.
Thomas Edmondson Land part of it processioned the Line Between Joseph Burnett & Thomas Bush.
Maybe William Dangerfield & John Chamberlain land not processioned they did not meet to have it processioned.
Thomas Wyat Land not procession^{ed} he said he did not know his bounds before he had it surveyed it.

       James Gatewood
       Thom^s: Burke

In pursuance of an order of Vestry for ye parish of South Farnham Wee being appointed processioners to procession ye several persons lands in our precinct do make our return as followeth:
All ye Lands in ye s^d precincts being quietly processioned except orphans land in ye presence of Robert Sp Coleman & John Burnett. Given under our hands.

       John Haile
       James Allen
       Henry Harper

[49]   [1751 Processioning]
Pursuant to an order of Vestry dated ye 27th day of August 1751 Wee have processioned ye lands as followeth: Viz^t:

Beginning ye Line between John Gatewood Isaac Gatewood and then between William Gatewood & Isaac Gatewood in presence of Thomas Roan & Edward Davis Witnesses. Then ye Line Between John Gatewood & William Gatewood then between John Gatewood and Thomas Cook in presence of Thom^s Roane & Edward Davis witnesses. The Line between John Gatewood & Philip Gatewood agreed & marked without us.

Then ye Lines Between Capt William Roan & Philip Gatewood.
Then ye Line Between Capt William Roan & Nichol^s Pamplin.
Then ye Line Between Capt: William Roan and Robert Johnson.
Then ye Line Between Capt William Roan and Robert Price.
Then ye line Between Capt William Roan and John Latane.
Then ye Line Between Capt William Roan and Saml: Gordons Widdow all ye above in presence of William Roan & Edward Davis witnesses.

Then ye Line Between James Gordons widdow & George Moody in presence of Matthew Thomas and John Moody witnesses. The Line Between Capt William Roan & James Upshaw agreed & mark'd without us. The Line Between John Latane & George Coleman agreed & marked. Given under our hands this twenty eighth day of March anno Domi 1752.
                                Forest Upshaw
                                John Latane

In obedience to an Order of Vestry held for South Farnham parish the 27th: day of August 1751 Wee the Subscribers have processioned the following persons Lands Viz^t: The Line Between Mary Byrom & Daniel Daley peaceably procession'd all the Lands in our Precincts being Orphans Lands or otherwise binding on orphans lands not being processioned on ye same acc^t.
                                William Edmondson
                                Benjamin Allen
                                Dan^{ll} Dayley

According to an Order of Vestry Wee ye Subscribers have processioned all the Land in our precinct Quietly & peaceably 1752.

Ambrose Jones
Jam^s: Banks

Pursuant to an Order of Vestry of South Farnham parish dated ye 27th: day of August 1751 Wee ye Subscribers being appointed processioners of the upper precinct of ye s^d: parish began ye 6th: day of January 1752 being accompanied with William Rennolds William Wattkins & Leonard Sale, Wee processioned the Line between Sarah Rennolds and Daniel Swillivan: and ye 12th instant being accompanied with Thoms Coleman John Hill William Wattkins Daniell Swillivan junr William Rennolds Samuell Cross & William Smether ye younger processioned the line between Daniell Swillivan & John Smether one of the processioners and ye line between Thomas Coleman & John Smether and ye line between William Rennolds & John Smether and the 18th instant being accompanied with Thoms Coleman William Rennolds Samuell Cross Isaac Gatewood John Hill & William Smether ye younger wee processioned ye lines between Thomas Coleman and William Rennolds and ye lines between Thomas Coleman & Isaac Gatewood and ye line between Leonard Hill one of y ^{e}processioners & Isaac Gatewood and ye line between Thoms Coleman & Leonard Hill and ye line between John Hill and Leonard Hill and ye 27th instant, being accompanied

[50]   [1751 Processioning]

accompanied with Thomas Coleman William Rennolds & Forest Upshaw processioned ye line between William Rennolds & Forest Upshaw present.

Richard Upshaw & William Upshaw junr Wee processioned ye line between Forest Upshaw & Isaac Gatewood & the line between Forest Upshaw & William Gatewood and the line between William Gatewood & Richard Upshaw and ye line between William Gatewood and Richard Upshaw and ye line Between William Rennolds & Hannah Upshaw and ye line between William Rennolds & John Upshaw and y^e line between William Rennolds & Richard Upshaw & Richd Upshaw & Sarah Rennolds and John Hill & Sarah Rennolds, and y^e 7th day of February 1752 being accompanied with Thom^s: Coleman & Sammuell Cross wee processioned y^e line between them and on y^e 11$^{th\text{\textquotedblright}}$ of February 1752 being accompanined with Thomas Waring Francis Waring William Wattkins Thomas Coleman & William Smether y^e Younger wee processioned y^e line Between Thomas Waring & William Watkins and so finished. Given under our hands this seventeenth day of March 1752.

          John Smether
          William Gatewood
          Leonard Hill

Truly Registered p^r John Vass Clk of ye Vestry
Octob^r: ye 15th: 1752 Examined by John Vass } Church
                Jno Clements } Wardens

****

[51] [1755 Processioning]
At a Vestry held for the parish of South Farnham at Mrs. Rebeckah Jones's Piscataway Ferry on the 29th day of July 1755.
  Present
  The Rev^d: Alexander Cruden
  William Dangerfield }
  James Webb   } Church Wardens

Nicholas Smith, William Covington, Francis Smith, William Roane, Isaac Scandret, John Clements, John Upshaw, Thomas Waring Gent^m
Henry Vass Appointed Clk of the Vestry

Pursuant to an order of Court for the County of Essex bareing date ye seventeenth[?] day of June Anno Dominy one thousand seven hundred fifty & five. Whereby it is Ordered that the Vestry of each parish within the said county divide their parishes into so many precincts as to them shall seem most convenient for processioning every particular persons lands in the several parishes and appoint the particular times for processioning, likewise appoint two intelligent honest freeholders at least of every precinct to see such processioned performed and take & return to the Vestry an acc^t of every persons lands they shall procession and of the persons present at the same and what lands in their precincts they shall fail to procession and of the particular reasons of such failure.

This present vestry so therefore divides the parish of South Farnham into twenty precincts.

And it is ordered that Rice Jones, John Wiley, and Thos Dunn or any two of them procession every persons lands in their precinct begining at the lower end of Essex County and run to the Gleab Creek form thence to M^r. Leonard Hills Quarters on the Dragon & make their return as the law directs beginning the tenth day of Novemb^r and to finish by the tenth day of Decemb^r and to make their return as the law directs.

Ordered that Joshua Boughton, John Smith, and Jam^s Medley Junr or any two of them procession every persons lands in their precincts begining at M^r. Leonard Hills Quarter on the Dragon from thence to Joshua Boughtons & so to the Dragon and from thence to M^{rs}. Adams Quarter on the River Side beginning the fifteenth day of Novemb^r and to finish by the fifteenth day of Decemb^r and to make their return as the law directs.

Ordered that Nicholas Smith Junr William Broocke and Henry Crutcher or any two of them procession every persons lands in their precinct begining at Joshua Boughtons from thence up to John Dickes from thence up to Wm Cheney on ye Dragon beginning the twentieth day of Novemb^r and to finish by ye twentieth day of Decemb^r and to make their return as the law directs.

[52]   [1755 Processioning]
Ordered that Capt. John Webb Mr. Leonard Hill and John Dunn or any two of them procession every persons lands in their precinct begining at M^{rs}: Adams Quarter on the River Side from thence to Capt Tylers Creek by John Youngs & so to the Back Road by Thom^s Cauthorns from thence do[w]n the said Road to Joshua Broughtons begining the twenty second day of November & finish by the twenty second day of December and to make their return as the law directs.

Ordered that John Edmondson John Minter and Samuel Piles or any two of them procession lands in their precinct begining at Coll Robinsons Quarter land by Thomas Cauthorn from thence to John Dykes from thence down the Mill Swamp to Piscataway Ferry so down the Main Road to Coll Robinsons Quarter old field begining the twenty sixth day of

Novemb^r & to finish by the twenty sixth day of Decemb^r and to make their return as ye law directs.

Ordered that Maj^r. Richard Tyler James Jones and William Loury or any two of them procession every persons lands in their precinct begining at Coll Robinsons Quarter land by Thos. Cauthorn from thence to the creek where John Philips once lived and all the land between the River and the Road to Piscataway Creek begining the twenty eighth day of Novemb^r and to finish by the first day of January & to make their return as the law directs.

Ordered that Thomas Broocke Thomas Cox & Francis Brisendine or any two of them procession every persons lands in their precinct begining at William Cheyneys on the Dragon from thence to the head of Covingtons Mill Swamp and down the Swamp to Co^{ll} Taylors Quarter landing from thence up the Road by Thos. Williamsons to William Cheneys begining ye third day of Decemb^r and to finish by ye twelfth day of January and to make their return as the law directs.

Ordered that James Boughon Thomas Williamson and William Gordon or any two of them procession every persons lands in their precinct begining at Capt. Benj^a Smiths Landing and so up Piscataway Creek to the Old Mill from thence along the Road to Mr. Jam^s. Webbs Ordinary begining from thence down the branch to the Dragon & to William Cheneys from thence to Capt. Benj^a. Smiths Land begining the fifth day of Decemb^r & to finish by the fifteenth day of January and to make their return as the law directs.

Ordered that Thomas Dunn Richard Brown and John Cox or any two of them procession every persons lands in their present begining at Mathews Bridge from thence to the Road & down the Road to Elliotts old field from thence to the head of the Dragon & down the Dragon to a branch below Jam^s. Finneys from thence up the sd branch to M^r. Webbs Ordinary and so along the Road to Mathews Bridge begining the tenth day of Decemb^r and to finish by the last day of January and to make their return as the law directs.

Ordered that Richard Gatewood Rhodes Greenwood George Newbill and Johnathan Dunn or any two [of] them procession every person lands in their precinct begining between the two branches of the Dragon from thence up to the Main Road that divideth Essex County from King & Queen County begining the twelth day of Decemb^r & to finish by the last day of January and to make their return as the law directs.

Ordered that John Edmondson Jam^s Banks and Ambrose Jones or any two of them procession every persons lands in their precinct begining at Hales Bridge from thence down the Road to the Long Reach Road from thence to the head of Fishers Mills Swamp and down the Swamp to Mathews Bridge from thence along the Road to the old mill from thence up the Swamp to Hales Bridge begining at tenth day of Novemb^r and to finish by the tenth day of Decemb^r and to make their return as the law directs.

[53] [1755 Processioning]
Ordered that Samuel Allin Ambrose Wright and William Cox or any two of them procession every persons lands in their precinct begining at Hales Bridge from thence to the Long Reach Road from thence up the Road to the dividing line of the County from thence to the head of Piscatua Swamp & down the Swamp to Hails Bridge beginning the fifteenth day of Novembr & to finish by the last day of Decemb^r and to make their return as the law directs.

Ordered that Capt. Thomas Edmondson William Smith and Thom^s Games or any two of them procession every persons lands in their precincts begining at Hardees Ferry on Hoskins Creek from thence to Piscataway Ferry and so down each creek to the River begining the twentieth day of Novemb^r and to finish by the twentieth day of Decemb^r and to make their return as the law directs.

Ordered that Thomas Bush Joseph Burnet and Robert Sp Coleman or any two of them procession every persons lands in their precinct between the Little Ferry on Hoskins Creek and Piscataway Ferry & up to Boughan Mill and up to Whites Run Bridge begining the twenty second day of Novemb^r and to finish by the twenty second day of Decemb^r and to make their return as the law directs.

Ordered that John Haile Jam^s. Allin and Henry Kid or any two of them procession every persons lands in their precinct between Boughans Mill and so across to Warings Mill and so up to Hails Bridge and so across to Warings Mill Swamp begining the twenty sixth day of Novemb^r and to finish by the twenty sixth day of Decemb^r and to make their return as the law directs.

Ordered that Capt Forest Upshaw Capt John Latane and Ambrose Gatewood or any two of them procession every persons lands in their precinct between Hails Bridge and Warings Mill Swamp up to the dividing line of Essex County from King & Queen County begining the twenty eighth day of Novemb^r and to finish by the first day of January and to make their return as the law directs.

Ordered that M^r. Isaac Scandrett James Reeves and William Broocke or any two of them procession every persons lands in the Mill Neck from John Armstrongs & so across to William Greenhill begining the third day of Decemb^r and to finish by the twelfth day of January and to make their returns as the law directs.

Ordered that William Edmondson Benjamin Allen and Thos Davis or any two of them procession every persons lands in their precinct between John Armstrong and William Greenhill and Co^{ll} Warings Mill and so across to Henry Tandys begining the fifth day of Decemb^r and to finish by the fifteenth day of January and to make their return as the law directs.

Ordered that John Fantleroy Jam^s Upshaw and John Hill or any two of them procession every person lands in their precinct between Co^l Warings Mill & Henry Tandys and so up to Charles Wallers from thence to M^r. Jam^s Rennolds begining the tenth day of December and to finish by the last day of January and to make their return as the law directs.

Ordered the Leonard Hill William Watkines and Isaac Gatewood or any two of them procession every person lands in the Upper Precinct to King & Queen begining the twelfth day of Decemb^r and to finish by the last day of January and to make their return as the law directs.

Mr. Leonard Hill appointed a vestryman for South Farnham Parish.

                    Sign'd
                    Alex^r Cruden
                    W^m. Daingerfield ⎫
                    Jam^s Webb   ⎬ Churchwardens

Truly registered p^r Henry Vass Clk of the Vestry

****

[54]   [1755 Processioning]
At a Vestry held for the Parish of South Farnham at M^{rs}. Rebeckah Jones's Piscataway Ferry May ye 31st 1756.
          Present
          The Revd Alex^r Cruden
          James Webb   Churchwarden

Francis Smith, William Covington, James Mills, Isaac Scandrett, John Upshaw, Gent.

Ordered that the Returns made by the Processioners be Truly Registered in the Vestry Book and that they be Exam^d over by the Vestry to se[e] that they be rightly entered within six months after the date hereof.
                    Alex^r Cruden
                    Jam^s Webb   C. warden

In obedience to any order of Vestry held for the parish of South Farnham in County of Essex dated the 29th day of July 1755 Wee the subscribers have processioned the lands as followeth Beginning at the lower end of Essex County processioned the line between Rice Jones & Samuel Mountague orphan between William Buford & Augustine Owen Between Augustine Owen & Charles Madearis, Between Augustine [Owen] & Thoms Taff Thomas Buford Augustine Owen Thos Taff present Between M^{rs}. Susanna Parker & Augustine Owen Between M^{rs}. Parker & Thomas Taff Between Lewis Mountague & John Massey & William Wood, Between John Massey & John Segar Augustine Owen Thos Taff Thos Clark Robt Clark Present.

Between John Massey & Reubin Shelton, Between Thomas Clark &

Reuben Shelton, Between Reuben Shelton & Josiah Martire Between
Reuben Shelton & James Richeson & Martin, Between James Richeson
& Abraham Mountague Between Abraham Mountague and Josiah
Martire, Between Abraham Mountague & Thomas Clark, Between Thom^s
Clark & John Massey. John Madearis Thos Clark present. Between John
Wiley & John Clark Between John Clark & M^{rs}. Parker Between John
Clark & John Bush Between John Bush & John Wiley Between John
Wiley & John Massey John Midearis & John Clark present.

Between Capt William Mountague & John Massey. Between John Massey
and John Bush. Between John Bush & Capt. William Mountague. Between
Abraham Mountague & Samuel Mountague Orphan. Between Samuel
Mountague Orphan & John Paine. Between M^r. Leonard Hill & John
Paine. Between Leonard Hill & Abraham Mountague John Bush John
Medearis William Paine present.

The line between Thos Dean & M^{rs}. Parker between John Bush and Thos
Dean. Between Thos Dean & Ab^r: Mountague. Between John Bush & M^{rs}.
Parker. Between M^{rs}. Parker & John Wiley, Thos Dean Evan Davis
Present.

Between Rice Jones & Augustine Owen the line between Rice Jones &
John Crowdas Between Rice Jones & M^{rs}. Susanna Parker the back line
between M^{rs}. Parker & John Croudas processioned nigh the corner the
corner not to be found nor the upper line John Croudas & Robt Clark
present.

[55]   [1755 Processioning]
Processioned the upper line between Capt William Montague and M^{rs}.
Parker the back line not to be found. Capt Montague prsent.
3 lines.   Ex^a Rice Jones
                                    John Wiley
                                    Thomas Dean

In obedience to an order of the gentlemen of the Vestry of South
Farnham parish bareing date the 29th day of July Anno: Dom: 1755 We
the Subscribers have processioned the lands in the precinct mentioned in

the s^d ord^r as followeth Viz^t

Begining November ye 24th processioned the lines between M^r. Thomas Hill & Joseph Sanderes between Joseph Sanders & James Medley jun^r Between James Meadley and M^r. Thos. Hill Between James Medley & Abraham Mountague Between James Medley & Capt William Beale Joseph Sanders & John Sanders present.

Processioned the lines between James Medley Senr & Capt. William Beale between James Medley & Vincent Vass. Between James Medley and the orphans of Charles Sanders dec^d James Meadley Senr & John Sanders present. November ye 25th: Processioned the lines between the Gleabe Land of South Farnham parish & Abraham Mountague between the Gleabe and M^r. Thomas Roane. Between the Honourable Richard Corban Esqr and Capt. William Beale. Between Capt William Beale & Thomas Roane Rev^d. M^r. Alex^r Cruden Henry Vass & John Newbill present.

December ye 9th. Processioned the lines between the Honourable Richard Corban Esqr & M^r. Richard Adams Between Capt William Beale & Vincent Vass James Femister and Thomas Coats present processioned the lines between Mr. John Armisted & Joshua Boughton Bewteen Joshua & John Boughton. Between John Boughton & the land said to belong to the orphans of Philemon Bird dec^d Between John Boughton & Vincent Vass Between John Boughton and Joseph Patterson Between John Armisted & John Boughton and Joseph Patterson Between John Armisted & John Boughton John Boughton jun^r present.

December ye 19th. Processioned the lines between John Armisted and Joseph Patterson. Between Joseph Patterson & John Smith. Between John Armisted and John Smith.

The following lines are not to be found Viz^t Between the River Side land of Capt. William Beale & M^r. Richard Adams. Between the Back Land of Capt. William Beale and M^r. Adams. Between M^r. Adams & Vincent Vass. Between Vincent Vass and Joseph Patterson.

Given under our hands this 15th day of Decembr 1755.
       John Smith
       James Medley jun^r

Pursuant to an order Vestry held for the parish of South Farnham the 29th day of July 1755. We the Subscribers have processioned the several persons lands in the precinct appointed us as follows Viz^t On the 20th day of November we began & processioned the line between Joshua Boughton & Vincent Hudson in presence of the parties of Philip Patterson. Also the line between Francis Smith & Samuel Broocke. Between said Smith & John Broocke, between said Smith and John Evans. Between said Evans and John Cheyney and

[56] [1755 Processioning]
The line between Francis Smtih & said Cheyney prsent. John Evans Pat: Lunan Meriwether Smith Philip Patterson. We also processioned the lines between Francis Smith & Wm Broocke Between said Smith & Henry Crutcher. Between the said Smith & Thomas Newbill Between ye said Smith & Shepards Orphans Between the said Smith & Edward Bomar present Philip Patterson & Patrick Lunan.

November 27. We processioned the lines between Mary Young & John Cheyney Between said Young & Eliza Johnson. Between John Cheyney & Nicholas Smith Present Thomas Johnson James Garner John Cheyney. Between Nicholas Smith & Henry Vass. Between Henry Vass & Edward Bomar. Present John Vass Peter Broocke & John Cheyney.

Decr 6th. We processioned the lines between Nicholas Smith & Saml Smith present Abner Dobynes also the lines between Thomas Newbil & Maberry Crutcher present Abner Dobyns & Henry Crutcher jun^r. Decr 13th. We processioned the lines between Thomas Newbill & Shepard orphans. Between said orphans & Thomas Broocke present Thomas Newbill Humphrey Davis & John Cheyney. 19th Decr. We processioned the line between Thoms Broocke & Fra^s. Brazindine between said Brizendine & Daniel Dobyns's heirs & Edward Bomar said Dobynes's Heirs & between said Bomar & Thomas Broocke present. Thos. Broocke Fra^s. Brizendine Edward Bomar & John Cheyney Also we processioned the line between Willm Broocke & Henry Crutcher present Philip Patterson W^m. Broocke Junr.   Ex^a Nicho^l. Smith Jr
                                                        William Broocke
                                                      Henry Crutcher

Gentlemen of the Vestry May ye 31st 1756
By a order of Vestry that Capt. John Webb M^r. Leonard Hill & I should procession the lands in our precinct Capt Webb being sick all the time & M^r. Hill Dead the return cannot be made by one alone. I am Gent^m your Hum^b Servt

    Ex^a John Dunn

In obedience to any order of Vestry we have procession$^{'d}$ the lands in the precinct therein mentioned as follows Viz^t Began at Coll^o Robinsons Quarter land accord^g s^d ord^r the lands of M^r. Jam^s. Webb Thos. Johnson & William Mitchell present s^d Johnson Mitchel & son Jacob also the line between the orphan of Isaac Mitchel & s^d Johnson & John Cauthan Henry Cauthan would not agree the line between him of s^d John Cauthan should be processioned, the lines between said John & Henry Cauthan the orphan of Isaac Mitchel & John Minter processioned also Richard Jeffries & Samuel Piles lands & the lands of Isaac Broocke & in the precinct in s^d ord^r. Mention^d as also the lands of James Jones Dec^d. Given und^r our hands this first day of December 1755.

    Ex^a John Evans
            John Minter

[57] [1755 Processioning]
Pursuant to an Order of Vestry held for the Parish of South Farnham on the 29th day of July 1756 We the Subscribers did proceed & have procession$^{'d}$ the Lands in our precinct has follows

Novr 28th We met at Coll^o. Robinsons Quart^r in order to procession the Lands of said Robinson but no person appeared to shew y^e Lines.

Decem^r. 5th We processioned the Lands between Col^l. Smith & Mess^r John & Willm Lowry. Between said Smith & James Cauthorn. Between said Smith & the orphans of Henry Young Deceas$^{'d}$. Between said Smith & John Webb on the side of Piscataway Creek on Francis Jones Vincent Cauthorn Thos. Lowry & Patrick Lunan.

Decemb^r 20th We procession$^{'d}$ the Lines between the Orphans of Henry Young dec^d and William Cauthorn. Between the orphans of W^{m}son Young Dece$^{'d}$ & said Cauthorn & a line between the orphans of Henry

Young dec^d & W^m son Young dec^d & between the orphans of Henry Young & John & Wm Loury in presence of W^m son Cauthorn & John Lowry. The other lands in our precinct we could not procession for want of the proprietors to shew us the lines.

         Richard Tyler
         James Jones
         William Lowry

Pursuant to an order of Vestry bareing date ye 3rd day of Decemb^r 1755 We the subscribers have peaceably & quietly processioned every persons lands in our precinct except the lines between Henry Purkins Tyler & Constantine Edmondson which said line cant be found without Philpar Edmondson. In the presence of William Cooper, James Oneale, John Vass, Stephen Neale, Charles Breadlove, John Mann, William W^m son, William Fletcher, Robert Acres, & John Roden. Given under our hands this 8th day of January 1756.

         Thomas Broocke
         Thomas Cox
         Francis Brizendine

In Obedience to an order of the Vestry of South Farnham Parish bareing date the 29th day of July 1756 We the subscribers have procession^d the lands of the respective persons in our precinct as followeth Viz^t. The line between Francis Brizendine & Thomas Cox processioned in the presence of John Brizendine & Thos. Cox. The line between the said Thomas Cox & John Brizendine processioned in the presence of the s^d Cox & Brizendine, the line between Robert Acres & the said Thomas Cox. Processioned in the presence of the said Cox & the aforesaid John Brizendine. The line between the said Robert Acres & Eliz^a Cooper processioned in presence of the said Robert Acres. The line between John Williamson & the said Eliz^a Cooper processioned in the presence of the said John Williamson and the aforesaid Robt. Acres. The line between the said John Williamson & John Davis processioned in the presence of the said Williamson & Davis.

[58] [1755 Processioning]
The line between James Webb & the said John Davis processioned the

presence of the said Davis & the afores^d John Williamson. The line between the said John Davis & John Shurdan's Orphans processioned in presence of the said Davis & the afores^d John Williamson. The line between Williamson & William Gordon processioned in the presence of the said Gordon. The line between James Turner & the said William Gordon processioned in the presence of the said Gordon by the consent of the said Turner. The line between Leonard Williamson & James Turner processioned by consent of the said Leonard Williamson & Jams Turner processioned by consent of the said Turner without his being present. The line between Leonard Williamson & Capt Peachey processioned. The line between Thomas Williamson & the s^d Peachey processioned. The line between the said Peachey & Benj^a Fishers Orphans processioned. The line between Berry Taylor & George Turner processioned in presence of the said Taylor.

The line between John Webb & James Turner processioned in presence of Berry Taylor. The line between the said James Turner and Leonard Williamson processioned. The line between the said James Turner & Capt Peachey processioned in presence of Thos Turner. The line between the said Peachey & John Tylor processioned. The line between the said Tyler & James Boughan processioned. The line between the said Tyler & James McCall processioned in presence of Arch^d McCall. The line between the said Tyler & Capt Peachey processioned. Given under our hands this 5th day of March 1756.

      Ex^a James Boughan
            Thomas Williamson
            William Gordon

Pursuant to an order of the Vestry of South Farnham Parish bearing date the 29th day of July Anno. Dom. 1755. We the Subscribers have processioned the Lands in our precinct as followeth Viz^t. The line between Berry Taylor & Ge^o. Turner processioned in the presence of John Britt & Berry Taylor. The line between Berry Taylor & Thos. Dennett in presence of Berry Taylor and Thomas Dennott. The line between Berry Taylor & Fran^s. Brown processioned in the presence of Francis Brown. The line between George Turner and Francis Brown in the presence of Francis Brown & John Brett. The line between Fran^s. Brown & Richard Brown in the presence of Rich^d. Brown and Francis Brown. The line between James Webb and Thomas Dunn processioned

in the presence of Thomas Dunn and James Webb. The line between
James Webb & Richard Brown in the presence of James Webb and
Richard Brown. The line between James Webb & John Dickerson
processioned in the presence of James Webb & John Dickerson.

[59]   [1755 Processioning]
The lines between Thomas Dunn and Richard & Francis Brown
processioned in the presence of Thomas Dunn and Richd & Frs Brown.
The line between Thomas Dunn and John Edmondson processioned.
The line between Thomas Dunn and Mary Marlow processioned in the
presence of Thos Dunn & John Edmondson.
The lines between John Edmondson and Thos Mason processioned in
the presence of John Edmondson and Thomas Mason.
The line between Thomas Mason & John Allens orphans processioned in
the presence of Thos Mason & John Edmondson.
The line between Thos Mason and Mary Marlow processioned in the
presence of Thomas Mason.
The line between Mary Marlow & John Allens orphans processioned in
the presence of James Dix & Mary Marlow.
The line between Thomas Miller & John Allens orphans processioned in
the presence of Thos Miller & James Dix.
The line between Jane Baker and John Allens orphans processioned in the
presence of Jane Baker & James Dix.
The line between Jane Baker & John Crow processioned in the presence
of Jane Baker & John Crow.
The line between William Crow and John Allen processioned in presence
of John Crow and James Dix.
The line between William Crow & Benj^a Dunn processioned in the
presence of John Crow & Benj^a Dunn.
The line between James Webb & Mary Marlow processioned in the
presence of James Webb and John Dickerson.
The line between Capt William Covington and John Dickerson in the
presence of Luke Covington and John Dickerson.
The line between Capt Wm Covington & James Webb processioned in
the presence of Luke Covington and James Webb.
The line between James Webb & Thos Edmondson processioned in the
presence of James Webb & Thomas Edmondson.

The line between James Webb and John Williamson processioned in the presence of Jaˢ Webb and Robert Williamson.
Given under our hands this 7ᵗʰ day of March 1756.

        pʳ Exᵃ   Thomas Dunn
                       Richard Brown
                       John Cox

In obedience to an order of Vestry bearing date ye 29ᵗʰ day July 1755 We the Subscribers have processioned the lands in our precinct as (viz)

The 16ᵗʰ day of Decembr Processioned John Harpers James Newbills Thomas Howertons Thomas Newbill Charles Addams prsent at the time.

17ᵗʰ Processioned William Greenwoods Rhodes Greenwoods George Newbills Isaiah Coles Robert Coles John Coles William Coles Richard Covington Robert Cole Wm Greenwood prsent at this time.

18ᵗʰ Processioned Thomas Simcoxs Wm Parris[?] Elizᵃ Staines's Richard Covingtons & part of Epraim Shepards and Richd Gatewoods Thos Crutcher Wm Turmans Part of Samuel Cooks's & part of Capt Wm Covingtons Thos Crutcher Wm Turman prsent at the time.

19ᵗʰ Processioned part of Joseph Mans John Townleys John Dishazo's Joseph Man junr John Townley prsent at the time. Mr. James Mills's land not processioned for want of some body to shew us th eline. James Femester's land not processioned for want of the line being shown. Mr Richard Shackelford's land not processioned for want of the line being shewn. Part of Lucy Purkins's part of Jams Coughland's. Part of Thos Howerton's not processioned because they joyn to Mr Shackelford's land. Given undʳ our hand this 10ᵗʰ day of Febr 1756.

                Exᵃ   Richard Gatewood
                          Rhodes Greenwood
                          George Newbill

[60]   [1755 Processioning]
In obedience to an order of Vestry held the 29ᵗʰ of July 1755, We the Subscribers have proceeded to procesion the land belonging to the

persons as follows (viz)

The line between Ambrose Jones & James Munday processiond by their consent, John Jones present. The land between Thos Dunn James Munday & William Dunn processioned by their consent. The line between William Dunn & John Tyler processioned by their consent. The line between James Munday & James Banks processioned by consent, William Dunn present.

The line between Doc[tr] John Clements & James Banks processioned by consent, William Ramsey present. The line between Ambrose Jones & Doctr Clements procesiond by consent, Henry Purkins prsent. The line between John Boughan & Henry Purkins procesiond by consent and between Henry Purkins Thomas Broocke & between Thomas Broocke Jacob Shearwood & Jonathan Radford by their consent. Each partie prsent. The line between Keziah Brown & Thomas Roane processiond by consent. The line between John Smith, John Farguson, Daniel Hodghill & John Croxton processiond by their consent. Each partie present. The line between Henry Brown Caty Gatewood & John Edmondson processiond by their consent. The line between Thomas Miller Elizabeth Allen & John Edmondson processiond by their consent being all the land in our precinct.

     Ex[a]   J. Edmondson
          James Banks } Present
          Ambrose Jones

In obedience to an order of Vestry for South Farnham Parish on the 29th day of July 1755 We the subscribers have processioned the land in our precinct as followeth

Novemb[r] 20th: the line between John Croxson & Hezekiah Brown procession'd in presence of Richard Hodges & Samuel Croxon. The line between James Bucker & William Fretwell procession'd in presence of the afores[d]. The line between Ambrose Wright & Thomas Miller and the line between William Fretwell and Thomas Miller. Processioned in the presence of Rich[d] Hodges and James Bucker. The line between Richard Jones & Richard Hodges procession'd in presence of Rich[d] Jones & John Jones. The line between John Clark & Rich[d] Jones ju[r] procession'd in presence of Richard Jones and Rich[d] Hodges. The line between Richard Jones & his son Rich[d] Jones processioned in presence of Richd Hodges & William Bennet.

Novemb[r] the 25th. The line between Richard Hodges & Richard Jones jur processiond in presence of William Bennet & Richd Jones. The line between Ambrose Wright & Richd Jones processiond in presence of Richard Hodges and James Wright and William Bennet. The line between Richard Hodges and Ambrose Wright processioned in presence of James Wright and William Benet. The line between Ambrose Wright & Thomas Croxton processioned in presence of Richd Hodges Thos Croxton & Jas Wright.

[61]   [1755 Processioning]
Novemb[r] 26th: The line between John Croxton & his son John Croxton processioned in presence of George Wright and Richard Hodges. The line between Richd Hodges and Josiah Minter processiond in presence of George Wright & John Croxton. The line between George Wright and Josiah Minter procession'd in presence of John Croxton and Richard Hodges. The line between George Wright & Richard Hodges procession'd in presence of Josiah Minter & John Croxton. The line between George Wright & John Croxton. The line between George Wright and Josiah Minter processioned in presence of John Croxton and Richard Hodges processioned in presence of Josiah Minter & John Croxton. The line between George Wright & Henry Cox processioned in presence of Richd Hodges John Croxton and Josiah Minter. The line between Henry Cox and John Pickett procession'd in presence of the afores[d]. The line between William Cox and Pickett & Between William Cox and Henry Cox processioned in presence of the afores[d]. The line between Sam[l]. Allen & Henry Cox processioned in presence of the afores[d].

Decemb[r] 1st. The line between John Ball and John Lumkin procession'd in presence of Joseph Reaves Jam[s] Ball Mark & Abner Ball. The line between James Ball and John Lumkin procession'd in presence of John Ball Joseph Reaves Mark & Abner Ball. The line between James St. John and Jam[s]. Ball processioned in presence of John Ball Mark & Abner Ball. The line between Joseph Ryland and Henry Cox procesion'd in presence of Georg Wright and William Allen. The line between Joseph Ryland and George Wright processioned in presence of Henry Cox & William Allen. The line between Joseph Reaves and John Latane processioned in presence of Thomas Coleman John and Edmond Ball. The line between Joseph Reaves & John Ball processioned in presence of John Latane & Thos Coleman. The line between John Latane and Henry Ball procession'd in presence of Thomas Coleman Mark Ball & Joseph Reaves. The line between John Latane and Mark Ball processioned in presence of Thos. Coleman and Joseph Reaves. The line between John Latane & Abner Ball processioned in presence of Joseph Reaves and Thomas Coleman. The line between Saml. Allen and John Harwood processioned in presence of William Allen Mark & Abner Ball.

M^r. Braxtons line not processioned the reason no body met to shew us the line.

Samuel Allen
Ambrose Wright
William Cox

I was not able to execute the above order in the time limited, therefore offer'd it to William Smith who refused to take it being removed out of the precinct.

Ex^a Thom^s Edmondson

[62] [1755 Processioning]
[this page is blank; probably this page was left blank for the return of precinct #14 which was never recorded]

[two unnumbered blank pages next]

[63] [1755 Processioning]
Pursuant to an order of Vestry to us directed we have been and processioned the lines of all the lands within our precinct as followeth (Viz^t) on Saturday ye 29th of Novr We went at the request of Robt Sp Coleman and mark'd the old line between the orphan of John Allen dec^d

on that part y^t was left by the old Widdow Allen and that part which ye s^d Coleman bought of Nathaniel Pendleton, begining at a Red oak starting by ye Forest Road to Dickes Mill & on ye westside ye s^d Colemans plantation. Thence about S^th along an old mark'd line to a red oak standing by ye Road about E by S^th to the s^d Coleman's Plantation wch he bought of Hugh Wilson where ye s^d Coleman objected to marking any line between him & the s^d Kemp untill they were better settled. So we went over to the line between ye s^d Coleman & the Orphans of Henry Reeves and mark'd some trees but ye said Coleman finding the line not mark'd on a direct course forbid us marking any further.

Then we went with M^r. Thos. Meddors & Robt. Sp Coleman on the line between & s^d Medder on the part they bought of Edwin Thacker & Doct^r John Clements on ye part that was Evanes begining at a large red oak now call^d the bluddy oak. Thence along an old mark'd line about N^th to an old line of the s^d Meddors now Nicholas Falkner to a hickory. Thence along the line between ye s^d Medder & the s^d Folkner about W^st over the Road to Medderses Bridge & so on to a white oak corner in ye s^d Meddorses old line on the west side a hill. Thence along a line between the s^d Medder & Eliz^th Wagener about S^th to a hickory corner of ye s^d Wagener.

Doc^r Clements and Robt Sp Coleman standing on the north side ye road to Daingerfields Mill. Thence we went at the request of ye s^d Coleman on the line between him on the land y^t was Pendletons & the s^d Wagener about west along the side of the s^d Wageners plantation to ye stump of an old pine standing at the head of a bottom near another large mark'd pine. Thence along another a line of the s^d parties about NW^st over 2 branches to a stake standing between two large red oaks on ye side a hill near ye s^d Wageners house. Thence along a line between ye s^d Coleman & the orphans of Thos Evans about S^th over the s^d two branches to the red oak mentioned. Between the orphans of Allen and the s^d Coleman standing by ye road afores^d and there we concluded for the day.

On Wednesday ye 3^d of Decem^r We met to procession the line between Doc^r John Clements & Robt Sp. Coleman on the parts y^t was Taylors when ye s^d Coleman finding the line not according to his mind objected to processioning it at which ye s^d Clements desired we would defer it untill he could make further enquirere & carried us on a line between him & the s^d Clements & the orphans of Henry Reeves on the part that was Taylors begining at some small bushes standing on a level in Colemans line on the southside ye s^d Clements's Plantation.

Thence along an old line about NE over a branch & across a road to ye Church, & down a valley by ye Church Spring but could find no corner. Robt Sp Coleman & his son Thos & the s^d Clements prsent.

[64]   [1755 Processioning]
The sd Clements say'd it would not signifie to procession the other line binding on Reeves's Orphans as no one appeared for them. Then we left them & went down on ye line between John Burnet Senr & John Burnet jun^r begining at a large white oak corner of Jo^s Burnet by ye road to Piscataway. Thence along an old mark'd line between their two plantations about S by E to Pettes's Plantation present young Benj^a Burnet for his fath^r & young John Burnet for himself.

Oliver Howard in favour to Pettis's orphans objected to processioning any line binding on ye land of ye s^d orphans, then we went on ye line between ye s^d John Burnet jun^r & y ^{e}land y ^{t}was Henry Harpers, now William Smiths, begining at a large read oak standing by a branch of Piscataway on ye E side ye s^d Smiths Plantation. Thence up ye s^d branch to a w^{ht} oak in Kemps line in ye presence of boath parties & Thos & Wm Burnet. Thence along Kemps line between him & Smith about S. Wst to a white oak standing in a branch in the line between ye s^d Kemp & John Hail present ye above mentioned persons & Jeremiah Burnet.

On Monday ye 8th of Decr at the request of Mr Jam^s Burnet we went on ye line between him & Robt Sp Coleman on ye part y^t was Hugh Wilsons begining at a large pine standing on ye top of hill on ye south side a branch of the Church Swamp in the old line that was formerly Ja^s. Taylors on ye south side of ye s^d Burnets Plantation, thence about NWst over the sd branch & by ye s^d Burnets Plantation to a large red oak corner thence along Burnets line to a white oak, his corner before mentioned standing by ye road to Piscataway. Thence along the line between Jn °Comp & young John Burnet by a large hickory corner by John Burnets house. Thence along an old line about SWst by W^m. Smith's plantation to a white oak in a branch of Piscataway & in John Hailes line before mentioned.

Thence up the branch about N^th to the line of the Orphans of John Allen dec^d at an old field and there were concluded that day.

On Tuesday day ye 9th of Decr We procession'd ye line between us John Haile & Jam^s. Allen begining at a corner hickory & Spanish oak in old Hailes now Latanes line by a branch of Piscataway. Thence NE over a ridge to another branch to another Spanish & pine. Thence down ye s^d branch to the line between M^r. Kemp & the orphans of John Allen at another branch to a beach. Present Henry Kid & Richd Hail. Then we went on the line between Henry Kid & John Latane on the part that was old Hails begining at a pine at the head of a branch of Piscataway. Thence about N^th to John Hails line on another of the s^d branches.

On Wednesday ye 6th of January we went on ye line between Elizabeth Waganer and William Medder begining at a w^ht oak by the path from the s^d Wageners to the s^d Meddorses. Thence about E^st over a branch of Hoskins Creek to a white oak corner of ye s^d Wagner & Thos. Medder on the west side a hill as before mentioned, present Reuben Wagener. We went by the request of Maj^r. Roane to procession ye line between him & the Widdow Bell but the s^d Roane fail^xd to attend so we did not mark the said line.

[65] [1755 Processioning]

We went on the line between Maj^r. Roane & Jam^s Allen begining at a pine by ye side of a branch by the side of s^d Roanes Plantation on ye part that was Thos Gatewoods. Thence down the s^d branch southwardly about a mile to a Spanish oak corner of John Hailes. The line between John Hails and William Smith a branch of Piscataway. The line between John Hail & Henry Kid a branch of Piscataway. The back lines of John Burnet, Pettis's orphans, Wm Smith, John Hail, Henry Kid, John Latane, within our precinct bounded by Piscataway Swamp, Cumtons land an orphans, John Allens land an orphans, Smiths land, binding on Wagner & Medder, an orphans, the land that was George Reeves's, an orphans.

Witness our hands   Ex^a   John Haile
                                       James Allen
                                       Henry Kid

Pursuant to an order of Vestry of South Farnham Parish dated the 29th day of July 1755 We have procession'd the lands in our precinct as followeth (viz)

Begining a line between John Gatewood and Isaac Gatewood and procession'd it according to law. Witness Thomas Roane, Philip Gatewood. Then between John Gatewood and William Gatewood. Witness Isaac Gatewood and Philip Gatewood.

Then between Maj^r. William Roane and Philip Gatewood. Witness John May. Then between Maj^r. Wm Roane and Nicholas Pamplin. Witness John Ray. Then between Maj^r. William Roane and Robert Johnson. Witness John Ray. Then between Maj^r. William Roane and Richard Lowry orphan, that the s^d Maj^r. Roane is gardian to. Witness John Ray & Robert Johnson. Then between Maj^r. William Roane and Capt. John Latane. Then between John Gatewood and Edward Davis. Witness Nicholas Pamplin and Thomas Barnes. Then between Maj^r. William Roane and Jane Gordon. Witness Edward Davis. Then between Jane Gordon and George Moody. Witness Edward Davis, Jeremiah Moody. Then between Thomas Dix and John Latane. Witness Tandy Dix. Then between Jane Gordon and John Latane.

     Ex^a Forest Upshaw
            John Latane
            Ambrose Gatewood

[66]   [1755 Processioning]
Pursuant to the within order of Vestry we the subscribers met once in order to procession the lands in the s^d order directed and Robert Sp. Coleman and James Griffing having some differences prevented us from proceeding and the time being expired in the s^d order rendered us uncapable of proceeding at another time.
     Ex^a Isaac Scandrett
            William Broocke
            James Reeves

In pursuance to an order of Vestry held for South Farnham Parish the 29th day of July 1755 We the subscribers have proceeded according to the sd order and procesion'd ye lands in our precinct as followeth (Vizt)

The line between Mr. Thomas Waring and Benjamin Waggener peaceably procession'd also the line between Co^ll. William Beverley and Benj^a Waggener peaceably procession'd also the line between Mary Davis and Mary Phitsimmon peaceably procesion'd. All other lands in our precinct belonging to orphans, therefore not procession'd. Given under our hands this 10th day of January 1756.

     Ex^a   William Edmondson
          Benj^a Allen

Pursuant to an order of South Farnham Parish vestry date the 29th day of July 1755 We the Subscribers have processioned the lands as followeth Viz

Begining January the 15th 1756 We processioned part of a line between Co^ll Francis Smith and M^r. John Fauntleroy, present the parties. Also W^m. Fauntleroy G^t, M^r. William Young, M^r. John Gordon, and Lachlen McIntosh. Then proceeding we processioned a line between Col^o Francis Smith and William Fauntleroy Gen^t present the parties. Also M^r. W^m. Young, M^r. John Gordon & Lachlen McIntosh, and George Nueman.

January the 16th. We processioned a line between William Fauntleroy G^m and Thomas Waring Gen^t present the parties. Also Mr John Gordon and George Newman. The remainder in our precinct we could not procession. The owners would not attend to shew their lines. Given under our hands this 31st day January 1756.

     Ex^a   John Fauntleroy
          James Upshaw
          John Hill

[67] [1755 Processioning]
Pursuant to an order of Vestry of South Farnham Parish dated ye 29th day of July 1755 Wee the subscribers being appointed processioners of the upper precinct of ye sd parish to King & Queen County began the 31st day of Decemb^r at a line between us the subscribers and being accompanied with John Hill, Richard Hill, Samuel Cross, Joseph Cross, and Alex^r Guill did procession the s^d line and the line between John Hill & William

Watkins, and the line between John Hill & Joseph Cross, then Samuel Cross & Joseph Cross left us, and then proceeded with the remainder of the company on a line between John Hill and Thomas Coleman, and the line between Leonard Hill & Thomas Coleman and a line between John Hill & Leonard Hill, the s^d Watkins at the request of the s^d Thomas Coleman, processioned ye said lines of the s^d Coleman.

January ye 5th We began at a corner of John Hills and being accompanied with John Hill John Upshaw John Smether Wm Rennolds & Jam^s Sullivant processioned the line between John Hill & Sarah Rennolds, William Rennolds in her stead, and the lines between Sarah Rennolds & Hannah Upshaw jun^r John Upshaw in behalf of the s ^{d}Upshaw, and a line between William Rennolds and old M^{rs}. Upshaw, the s^d John Upshaw in her behalf.

January ye 26th. Processioned a line between Francis Waring and William Watkins, the s^d Waring present.

January ye 27th. We began at a corner between John Upshaw and William Gatewood & being accompanied with John Upshaw, William Gatewood, William Rennolds & Thomas Cooper Dickenson Processioned the line between the s^d John Upshaw and William Gatewood, and the line between the s^d M^r. Gatewood and old M^{rs}. Upshaw, the s^d Dickenson left us and Isaac Gatewood present. Processioned the lines between old M^{rs}. Upshaw and William Rennolds & a line between M^{rs}. Upshaw and Isaac Gatewood and a line between Isaac Gatewood and Leonard Hill.

January ye 30th. Processioned a line between Richard Holt & Wm Watkins, the s^d Holt being present. All the other lands not processioned for want of the owners to shew their lines. Given und^r our hands this 31st day of January 1756.

          Leonard Hill
          Wm Watkins
          Isaac Gatewood

Truly Registered pr Henry Vass Clk of the Vestry
Novemb^r ye 2^d Examined by

[68]   [1755 Processioning]
At a Vestry held for South farnham Parish at Mrs. Rebeckah Jones's Piscataway Ferry 2^d day Novemb^r 1756

Present Revd Alex^r Cruden Wm Daingerfield & Jam^s Webb Churchwardens Nicho: Smith Wm Covington Franc^s Smith Wm Roane Jam^s Mills Thos Waring John Clements, John Upshaw Gent^m.

Then the Gentlemen of the Vestry met to Examine whither the returns made by the pcoessioners where [were] justly and truly entered in the Book appointed by ye Vestry for that purpose within the time as the law directs and do find the sd returns to be truly entered.

       Sign^d
       W Dangerfield
       James Webb

Truly Registered p^r Henry Vass Clk of ye Vestry

****

At a Vestry held for the Parish of South Farnham at M^{rs}. Rebeckah Jones's Piscataway Ferry ye 9th day of July 1759.
 Present
 The Revd Alex^r Cruden
 Fran^s Smith Churchwarden

William Daingerfield, William Covington, Jam^s Webb, John Upshaw, Isaac Clements, Wm Mountague and Wm Young Gent^m.

Pursuant to an order of Court for the County of Essex County bareing date ye 29th day of June Anno Dom^y. one thousand seven hundred fifty nine. Whereby it is ordered that the Vestry of each parish within the said county divide their parishes into so many precincts as to them shall seem most convenient for processioning every particular persons lands in the several parishes and appoint the particular times for processioning, likewise appoint two intelligent honest freeholders at least of every precinct and take and return to the vestry an acc^t of every persons lines they shall procession, and of the persons present at same and what lands in their precincts they shall fail to procession and of the particular reasons of such failure.

This present Vestry do therefore divide the Parish of South Farnham into twenty precincts and it is ordered that Robert Clerk, Thomas Clark, and Abraham Montague or any two procession every persons lands in their precinct begining at the lower end of Essex County and run to the Gleab Creek form thence to M^r. Leonard Hills Quarters on the Dragon & make their return as the law directs beginning the tenth day of Novemb^r and to finish by the tenth day of Decemb^r and to make their return as the law directs.

2nd Ordered that Joshua Boughton John Smith and Jam^s Medley Junr or any two procession every persons lands in their precincts begining at M^r. Leonard Hills Quarter on the Dragon from thence to Joshua Boughtons & so to the Dragon and from thence to M^{rs}. Adams Quarter on the River Side beginning the fifteenth day of Novemb^r and to finish by the last day of the same month to make their return as the law directs.

[69] [1759 Processioning]
3rd It is ordered that Nicholas Smith Henry Crutcher and Thomas Newbill or any two procession every persons lands in their precinct begining at Joshua Boughtons from thence up to Mr. James Webbs Quarter on the Old Mill Swamp that leads to Piscatawy Creek from thence to William Cheneys on the Dragon beginning the twentieth day of Novr and to finish by ye twentieth day of Decr and to make their return as the law directs.

4th It is ordered that Samuel Peachey Gent John Dunn and John Broocke or any two procession every persons lands in their precinct begining at M^{rs}: Adams Quarter on the River Side from thence to Maj^r Richard Tylers Creek by John Youngs & so to the Back Road by Thomas Cauthorns from thence down the said Road to Joshua Broughtons begining ye twenty second day of Nov^r & finish by the twenty second day of Decr and to make their return as the law directs.

5th It is ordered that John Evans Junr John Minter and Samuel Piles or any two procession lands in their precinct begining at Coll Robinsons Quarter land by Thomas Cauthorn from thence to Mr. James Webbs Quarter Land on the Old Mill Swamp thence down the said Swamp to Piscataway Ferry so down the Main Road to Coll Robinsons Quarter old field begining the twenty sixth day of Nov^r & to finish by the twenty sixth day of Decr and to make their return as ye law directs.

6th It is ordered that Maj^r. Richard Tyler Tscharner Degraffendreight and James Jones or any two procession every persons lands in their precinct begining at Coll Robinsons Quarter land by Thos. Cauthorn from thence to the creek where John Philips once lived and all the land between the River and the Road to Piscataway Creek begining the twenty eighth day of Novr and to finish by the first day of January & to make their return as the law directs.

7th It is rdered that Thomas Broocke Thomas Cox & Francis Brisendine or any two of them procession every persons lands in their precinct begining at William Cheyneys on the Dragon from thence to the head of Covingtons Mill Swamp and down the Swamp to Co^{ll} Tayloes Quarter landing from thence up the Road by Thos. Williamsons to William Cheneys begining ye third day of Decr and to finish by ye twelth day of January and to make their return as the law directs.

8th It is ordered that Philip Kid William Dunn jun^r and William Gordon or any two procession every persons lands in their precinct begining at Capt. Benj^a Smiths Landing and so up Piscataway Creek to the Old Mill from thence along the Road to Mr. James Webbs Orindary from thence down the branch to the Dragon & to William Cheneys from thence to Capt. Benjamin Smiths Landing begining the fifth day of Dec^r & to finish by the fifteenth day of January and to make their return as the law directs.

9th It is ordered that Thomas Dunn Thomas Dennet and Richard Brown or any two procession every persons lands in their precinct begining at Mathews Bridge from thence to the Road & down the Road to Elliots old field from thence to the head of the Dragon & down the Dragon to a branch below James Finnies from thence up the s^d branch to M^r. Webbs Ordinary and along the Road to Mathews Bridge beginning the tenth day of Decr and to finish by the last day of January and to make their return as the law directs.

10th　It is ordered that Rhodes Greenwood Richard Greenwood and George Newbill or any two procession every person lands in their precinct begining between the two branches of the Dragon from thence up to the Main Road that divideth Essex County from King & Queen County begining the twelth day of Dec^r & to finish by the last day of January and to make their return as the law directs.

[70]　[1759 Processioning]
11th　It is ordered that John Edmondson Jam^s Banks and James Boughan or any two procession every persons lands in their precinct begining at Hales Bridge from thence down the Road to the Long Reach Road from thence to the head of Fishers Mills Swamp and down the Swamp to Mathews Bridge from thence along the Road to the old mill from thence up the Swamp to Hales Bridge begining at tenth day of Novr and to finish by the tenth day of Decr and to make their return as the law directs.

12th　It is ordered that Samuel Allen Ambrose Wright and William Cox or any two procession every persons lands in their precinct begining at Hales Bridge from thence to the Long Reach Road from thence up the Road to the dividing line of the County from thence to the head of Piscataway Swamp and down the Swamp to Hales Bridge beginning the fifteenth day of Nov^r & to finish by the fifteenth day of Decr and to make their return as the law directs.

13th　It is ordered that Ambrose Jones, Thomas Games, and Charles Brey or any two procession every persons lands in their precinct begining at Hardees Ferry on Hoskins's Creek from thence to Piscataway Ferry and so down each creek to the River begining the twentieth day of Novr. to finish by the twentieth day of Decr and to make their return as the law directs.

14th　It is ordered that Thomas Burk, Joseph Burnet, and John Boughan or any two procession every person lands in their precinct between the Little Ferry on Hoskins Creek and Piscataway Ferry and up to Boughans Mill and up to Whites Run Bridge begining the twenty second day of Novr to finish by the twenty second day of Decr and to make their return as the Law directs.

15th   It is ordered that James Allen, Henry Kid, and Ambrose Gatewood or any two procession every persons lands in their precinct between Boughans Mill and across to Warings Mill and up to Hales Bridge and across to Warings Mill Swamp begining the twenty sixth day of Novr to finish by the twenty sixth day of Decr and to make their return as the law directs.

16th   It is ordered that Capt John Latane, Isaac Gatewood, and Vincent Vass or any two procession every persons lands in their precinct between Hales Bridge from King & Queen County begining the twenty eighth day of Nov^r & to finish by the first day of January and to make their return as the law directs.

17th   It is ordered that Robt Sp Coleman, James Reaves, and William Broocke or any two procession every persons lands in the Mill Neck from John Armstrong across to William Greenhill begining the third day of Decr to finish by the twelfth day of January and to make their return as the law directs.

18th   It is ordered that William Edmundson, Benjn. Allen, and John Davis or any two procession every persons lands in their precinct between John Armstrongs and William Greenhills and Co^{ll} Warings Old Mill and so across to Henry Tandys begining the fifth day of Decr to finish by the fifteenth day of January and to make their return as the law directs.

19th   It is ordered that James Upshaw, John Hill, and Sylvanus Tandy or any two procession every persons lands in their precinct between Coll Warings Mill and Henry Tandy's and up to Charles Wallers form thence to Mr James Rennolds's begining the tenth day of Decr to finish by the last day of January and to make their return as the Law directs.

20th   It is ordered the Leonard Hill William Watkins and Richd Hill Junr or any two procession every person lands in the Upper Precinct to King & Queen begining the twelfth day of Decr and to finish by the last day of January and to make their return as the law directs.

****

[71]   [1759 Processioning]
At a Vestry held for the Parish of South Farnham at M^{rs}. Rebeckah Joness Piscataway Ferry on the 24th day of Novr 1760

Present William Montague Church Warden
Francis Smith William Covington James Webb John Clements John Upshaw and Wm Young Gent^{mn}.

It is ordered that the Returns of the Processioners be truly Registered in the Vestry Book appointed for that Purpose and that they be Examined over at the next Vestry to see if they be Rightly Entered.
John Clements
William Montague

Pursuant to an order of the Vestry of South Farnham Parish dated the 9th day of July 1759 We the subscribers being two of the three that were appointed have processioned the several lands as followeth

Begining on the 10th day of Novr 1759 it being the day appointed to begin at the Low^r end of the County and processioned the line Between Mr. Lewis Montague and Robert Clark Present Mr. Lewis Montague. Novr 15th then Processioned the line between Mr. Lewis Montague and John Medeares Prest John Medeares.
Between John Cornelious and John Medeares the same present.
Between Thos Clark and John Medeares the same prsent.
The line between Reuben Shelton & Thos Clark Josiah McTyor prsent.
The line between Josiah McTyor and Thos Clark Josiah McTyor present.
The line between Josiah McTyer and Reuben Shelton Josiah McTyer prest.
The line between Reuben Shelton and Henry Street, Josiah McTyer prest.
The line between Henry Street & Jos^h Mactyer prest Jos^h Mactyer.
The line between Hen: Street & Abm: Montague Richd Street prest.
The line between Josiah Mactyer & Abraham Montague the same prest.
The line between Thos Clark & Abra Montague the same prest.

Novr 23^d
The line between Capt Wm Montague Mill acre of ground and Rice Jones an orphan, present Capt William Montague.
The line between Samuel Montague an orphan and Rice Jones an orphan present John Jones.
The line between Rice Jones an orphan and John Clowdas John Jones prest.
The line between Rice Jones an orphan & Augustine Owen John Jones prsent.
The line between Augustine Owen & Charles Medearses Augustine Owen present.
The line between Augustine Owen and Thos Taff. Present.

Novr 24th
The line between Thomas Bridgforth and Susanna Parker Titus Farguson and John Clark present.
The line between Susanna Parker and John Clark the same present.
Between John Clark and John Bush the same Prest.
Between John Bush & Susanna Parker Jn°. Bush Junr present.
Between John Bush and Thos Dean the same prest.
Between John Bush and Thos Bridgforth the same prest.

Novr 27th
Between Capt William Montague & Robert Clark Thomas Lee present.

[72]   [1759 Processioning]
Between Capt. William Montague & John Bush. the same present.
Between Capt. William Montague & William Amis. John Bush present.
Between Wm Amis & Leonard Hills orphans. the same present.
Between William Amis and Abraham Montague. John Bush and Abraham Montague present.
Between Abraham Montague & Benjamin Dean. Thomas Lee and Benj^a Dean prest.
Between Abra. Montague and John Bush. Prest Thos Lee & Richd Bush.
Between Abraham Montague and Thos Dean. Thos Dean & Benj^a Dean present.
Between Susanna Parker and Thos Dean, Thos Dean Benj^a Dean pres^t.
Between Thos Dean and Benjamin Dean, both parties present.

Decr 8th
The line between Susanna Parker and Rice Jones an orphan Jn°. Clark Pres.^t^
Between Susannah Parker & Thomas Taff, John Clark present.
Between Augustin Owen & Susannah Parker, the same present.
The line between some lands that Susannah Parker purchased in her widowhood and some other lands that she holds by a right of dower which John Armistead has conveyed to Capt W^m^. Montague, John Clark present.
No line to be found nor none shone between Susanna Parker and John Clowdas.

as Witness our hands this 20th day of Decr 1759
                              Robert Clark
                              Thomas Clark

In obedience to the Gentlemen of the Vestry of South Farnham Parish Essex County we the subscribers have processioned the bounds of each mans land in our precinct as followeth Viz

Novr ye 15. Processioned the line between Widdow Smith and Robt Hunley in the presence of James Medley Junr
Processioned the line between Robert Hunley and James Medley Junr in the present of Robt Hundley.
Processioned the line between Robert Hunley and James Medley Junr in the presence of Robt Hunley.
Processioned the line between James Medley Junr and Abraham Montague in the presence of Abraham Mountague.

Novr 16. Processioned the line between Joshua Boughton and Alex.^r^ Sanders in the presence of William Young and Vincent Hudson.
Processioned the line between John Boughton and Alexander Sanders in the presence of Joseph Paterson and Vincent Hudson.
Processioned the line between Widdow Smith and James Smith in the presence of Hudson and John Boughton.

Novr 22. Processioned the lines of James Medley Senr in the presence of Thomas Hunley.

Processioned the lines between John Boughton Senr and Joseph Patterson in the presence of Thomas Hundly. Processioned the line between M^r. Beale and James Medley Senr in the prsence of Robert Hunley, also the line between Mr Leonard Hill dec^d and Jam^s Medley Junr, also the line between the s^d Mr Hill dec^d and Robt Hunley in the presence of Jam^s Medley and Robert Hunley, also the line between James Medley and Abraham Montague in the presence of Jam^s Medley and Abra. Montague, also the line between the Gleab and Alex. Montague in the presence of Thos Watts and Abra. Montague, also the line between Capt Thos Roane Gen^t and Abra. Montague Thos Watt and Abra. Montague present, also the line between the Gleab and Capt Roan in the presence of Jam^s Medley also the line between Capt Roane and Thos Beale in the presence of Jams Medley & Thos Coats.

[73]   [1759 Processioning]
Also the line between Thomas Beale and Col^l. Corbin in the presence of Thos. Coats and Ambrose Calton. Also the line between Col^l Corbin and M^r. Adames in the presence of Thos Coats and Ambrose Calton. The line between M^r. Beale and M^r. Adams is not to be found.

        Joshua Boughton
        John his I mark Boughton

In pursuance to an order of Vestry held for the Parish of South Farnham the 9th day of July 1759 We the subscribers have processiond all the land in our precinct as follows

Novr. ye 20. 1759. Then processiond the land of Col^l Fran^s Smith in the presents of Wm Broocke Thos Broocke Vincent Hudson Philip Paterson.

dec^r. 4 1759. Then processiond the land John Cheyney in the presents of Ralph Neal Grifton Johnson Godfrey Young.

dec^r y^e 7th 1759. Then processiond the land of William Shepard in y^e presents of Wm Cheyney and John Cheyney.

dec^r y^e 13th Then processioned the land of Ralph Neal, Andrew Allen Th$\~o$ Broocke Ruben Dobbins and Thomas Dobbins dec^d orphans in y^e presents of James Johnson James Cooper and Edward Bomar. Then processioned the land of Edward Bomar in the presents of James Johnson.

Decr y^e 14th 1759 Then processioned the land of Nicholas Smith John Blatt Henry Crutcher Thos Newbill Wm Broocke in the presents of William Bomar Henry Cooper Henry Crutcher Junr John Owen Philip Broocke.

Then processiond the land of Vincent Hudson in the presents of John Boughton, Alex^r Sanders.

Nicholas Smith
Thomas Newbill

Pursuant to an order of the Vestry of South Farnham Parish dated the 9th day of July 1759 We the subscribers began to Procession the 29th of Novr and Processioned the line between M^r. Adams and Bird orphan Wm Boughton and John Patterson present no head line to be found to M^r. Adams land.

Decr 6th. Processioned the line between Mr. Adams & George Russell, Russell present. Between William Montague & Bird, Wm Boughton Pst. Between Isaac Williams and Joshua Boughton, said Williams and William Bough[t]on present. Between said Williams and Vincent Hudson, s^d Williams and George Russell present.
Between John Broocke and Sam Broocke both present.
Between Wm Broocke and Sam, John and Sam present.

Decr 7 Processiond the line between John Dunn and John Evans Greensby Evans present. Between said Dunn and John Evans Junr one of the s^d Evans's sons present. Between said Evans and Sarah Mitchell their sons present. Between Samuel Peachey and George Russell, latter prest.

Decr 13 Processiond the line between Capt Webb and John Evans s^d Webb and Greensby Evans prest. Processiond the line between Mr Hill and John Evans Junr, said Evans prest. Between said Evans and Philips orphans, said Evans and Richard Fisher prest. Between Saml Peachey and Philips orphans Ric^d Fisher prest. Between said orphans and George Russell, Fisher prest. Between said orphans and William Montague, Richd

Fisher prest. Between s^d orphans and Sam Broocke, Richd Fisher pres. Between Saml Peachey and Mr Hill, Peter Broocke prest. Between said Hill and Capt Webb and Broocke prest. Between said Webb and John Young orphans said Webb and Richd Faulkner prest. Between said Webb and Capt Gatewood, s^d Webb prest.

[74]   [1759 Processioning]
Between Mrs Young and said Gatewood, Wm Young her son prest. Between Mrs Young and John Evans said Wm Young and Micajah Evans Prest. No one to shew the line between Mr Hill and John Evans. The line between Wm Montague and George Russell there being a dispute about it wch they intent to settle peaceably between themselves.

      Samuel Peachey
      John Dunn
      John Broocke

In obedience to the within order we the subscribers have processioned all the Land in said order mentioned except Edmond Mitchell an orphan and the line between Richd Gatewood dec^d and Richard Jeffries s^d Jeffries absolutly refusing to allow s^d line to be processioned. Given under our hands this 26th day of dec^r 1759.

      John Minter
      Samuel Piles

In obedience to an order of Vestry Dated the 9th day of July 1759 We the subscribers have processioned the Lands in our Precinct as Follows. (Viz)

We met the 28th of Novr at the line dividing the Lands of Capt Richd Gatewood lately Coll^o Robinsons land the orphans of Williamson Young dec^d but could not proceed. The Parties claiming that Land not being prest to shew us the lines.

On Wednesday Decr the 5th we met at Col^o Fran^s Smiths and processiond the lines between said Smith and George Clayton, Wm Young, James Cauthorn, Vincent Cauthorn, Smith Young and William Lowry Prest. Other than the parties Isaac Broocke Robt Greer Vincent Cauthorn James Cauthorn Meriwether Smith, John Edmondson Junr George Bird and John Webb Junr.

Likewise the line between Smith Young and the orphans of John Lowry dec^d in presence of the above and Col^o Fran^s Smith.

We also processiond the line between James Cauthorn and Vincent Cauthorn, between Wm Young and said Cauthorn, between said Young and James Webb Junr, between said Young and John Richards. Between said Young and George Clayton also between said Young and Harwar Owens. The other lands in our precinct the parties claiming failing to appear to shew us the lines. We could not proceed to procession.

       Tscha^r. Degraffenried
       James Jones

Decr 3^d Begining on William Chaneys line also a line of Thos Coxes Ju^r also a line of John Oneal, also the line of Fran^s Brezendine in presents of William Chaney. Also the line of William Coles, also the line of the orphan of Bushses, also the line of John Vass's, also the line of Richd Johnsons, also the line of Robt James, also the line of Robt Man, also the line of Peter Tribles, also the line of Thomas Coles, also the line of Nathan Breadlove, also the line of the orphan of Tribles, also the line of Joseph Mans, also the line of Francis Jones, also the line of James Edmondson as Isaac Hays lives on, also the line of Constant Edmondson, also the line of Philip Kid, also the line of Thos Cox in the presents of John Mann. Also the line of Robt Acres, also the line of James Webb shoemaker.

[75]   [1759 Processioning]
Also the line of John Roden in the presents of Richard Cooper.
Also the line of Eliz^a Byrom, also the line of William Flitcher, also the line of Thomas Williamson in the presents of Ezekiel Byrom.
Also the line of William Gordons, also the line of John Davis, also the line of William Watkins in the presents of William Gordon.
All the Land in our precincts peaceably processioned by
       Thomas Cox
       Thomas Broocke
       Francis Brezendine

Pursuant to an Order made ye 9th day of July 1759 We the said Subscribers have processioned the sd lines.

The line between Thos Cox and John Brezendine processioned in presence of Thos Cox. The line between Thos Cox and Robt Acres, also the line between Eliza Cooper and John Williamson, also the line between John Williamson and John Davis, also the line between Mr Webb and John Davis, also the line between John Davis and John Shurdan's orphans, also the line between John Hays and James Turner, also the line between James Turner and Leonard Williamson, also the line between Leonard Williamson and William Gordon. The said lines all processioned in presence of Thos Cox.

Also the line between William Gordon and James Turner processioned in presence of James Turner. Also the line between James Turner and Leonard Williamson, also the line between Capt Benja Smith and James Turner, also the line between Benja Smith and William Dunn, also the line between Benja Smith and William Ramsey, als[o] the line between William Ram[s]ey and John Diggs, also the line between Arch{d} McCall and Wm Ramsey. All these lines processioned in presence of James Turner.

The line between Mr Tate and Mr Digs, the line between Mr McCall and Abner Cox processioned in presence of William Ramsey. The line between Abner Cox and Benja Smith, also the line between Capt Benja Smith and William Ramsey processioned in presence of John Hammon, also the line between Capt Smith and Benja Fisher orphan processioned in presence of Thos Williamson. The line between Thomas Williamson & Leonard Williamson processioned in presence of Thos Williamson. The line between Wm Gordon and Thos Williamson procesioned in presence of Thos Williams[on]. All the land in our precinct peaceably processioned.

         William Gordon
         William Dunn junr
         Philip Kidd

[76] [1759 Processioning]
Essex County South Farnham Parish
Pursuant to an Order of Vestry bearing date the ninth day of July 1759 We the subscribers have processioned the several persons lands in our

precinct as followeth (viz)

Jany 14 1760
The line between Thos Dennet and Berry Taylor processioned in the presence of the s^d Donnet and Taylor and William Ramsey.
The line between James Webb and Richard Brown in the presence of the s^d Webb and Brown.
The lines between James Webb and John Dickerson in the presence of the s^d Webb and Dickerson.
The line between James Webb and Mary Marlow in the presence of the s^d Webb and Wm Dunn Junr.
The line between Wm Covington and John Dickerson in the presence of the said Dickerson and Luke Covington.
The line between Drury Dobbins and John Brizendine in the presence of Hester Dobbins.
The line between James Webb and Drury Dobbins in the presence of James Webb and Luke Covington.
The line between James Webb and John Williamson in the presence [of] s^d Webb and Williamson.
The line between Francis Brown and Berry Taylor in the presence of Wm Ramsey and Berry Taylor.
The line between Thomas Dunn and Francis Brown processioned in the presence of William Ramsey.
The line between Thos Dunn and Richard Brown processioned in the presence of William Ramsey.
The line between Thomas Dunn and Mary Marlow processioned in the presence of William Ramsey.
The line between Thomas Dunn and Thomas Mason processioned in the presence of Thos Mason and Wm Ramsey.
The line between Benj^a Dunn and Susanna Crow processioned in the presence of Benjamin Dunn and Philip Dunn.
The line between Susanna Crow and Elizabeth Allen in the presence of Benja Dunn Phill Dunn and William Marlow.
The line between Eliza Allen and Jean Baker in the presence of Benjamin Dunn Phill Dunn and William Marlow.
The line between Elizabeth Allen and Thomas Miller in the presence of Benj^a Dunn Phill Dunn & Wm Marlow.
Given under our hands this 31st day of January 1760.

Thomas Dunn
Thomas Dennet
Richard Brown

Pursuant to an Order of the Vestry of the Parish of South Farnham we the subscribers have processioned the several bounds of land in our precinct.

Begining on the line between Rhodes Greenwood and Isaiah Cole the s^d Greenwood and Cole being present.
Between Robt Cole and Wm Greenwood, both parties present.
Between Isaiah Cole and Robert Cole, both present.
Between John Harper and James Newbill, both present.
Between John Harper and Thos Howerton, both present.

[77]   [1759 Processioning]
Between Thomas Howerton and Heritage Howerton, both present.
Between Heritage Howerton and Obediah Howerton, both present.
Between Obediah Howerton and William Howerton, both present.
Between Wm Howerton and John Howerton, both present.
Between William Howerton and Richard St John, both present.
Between William Covington and Samuel Coats, the sd Coats Luke Covington present.
Between William Tureman and Thos Crutcher, both present.
Between Wm Tureman and Jonathan Dunn, both present.
Between Isaac Kidd and John Crow, both present.
Between Arthur Tate and James Newbill, the sd Newbill, Samuel Coats, and James Atkins prsent.
Between Ja^s Newbill and George Newbill, both present.
Between Ja^s Newbill and Samuel Coats, both present.
Between Richard Gatewood and Richard St John, the sd St John and Robert Cole present.
Between Richard Covington and Arthur Tate and between the said Covington and Robert Cole, the said Covington and Cole present.
Between William Greenwood and Arthur Tate, the sd Greenwood present.
Between Richard Covington and William Parr, both present.
Between Richard Covington and Ephraim Shepard, both present.

Between John Howerton and Richd St John, both present. Between Roger Shackleford and Richard St John and between the sd Shackleford and Heritage Howerton and between the sd Shackleford and Thomas Howerton. Between the sd Shackleford and John Harper, all in the presence of the sd Roger Shackleford, Richard St John and Obediah Howerton.

Between Roger Shackleford and Arthur Tate, the said Shackelford and James Atkins present.
Between the said Shackleford & William Watkins, the said Shackleford and Watkins present.
Between Samuel Coats and Arthur Tate, the s^d Coats & Ja^s Atkins present.
Between Samuel Coats and Thomas Crutcher, the said Samuel Coats Henry Crutcher and Thomas Crutcher present.
Between the sd Crutcher and William Covington, the said Crutcher and Luke Covington present.
Between Joseph Mann and James Cauthorn, the sd Cauthorn Isaac Kidd and Samuel Coats Junr present.
The bounds of the lands belonging to John Townly, Thomas Simcoe dec^d and John Cole are not processioned there being nobody to shew the lines.
Richd Gatewood refused to have the line processioned between himself and John Howerton he not being able to attend.

Rhodes Greenwood
William Greenwood
George Newbill

In obedience to any order of Vestry bearing date the 9th of July 1759 We the subscribers have processioned the land in our precinct as followeth Viz

The line between John Edmondson Thomas Dunn Thos Dunn and James Munday James Munday and William Dunn James Munday and James Banks proecesioned by consent of each partie, Wm Dunn Junr present.

Between John Clements and James Banks in their presence Arthur Tate present.
Between James Munday and James Boughan by their consent.
Between s^d Boughan and John Jones by their consent.

[78]   [1759 Processioning]
Between James Booker and John Edmondson by consent each partie present.
Between Caty Gatewood and Henry Brown by consent.
Between James Booker and Thomas Miller by consent, Booker present.
Between Henry Purkins and John Boughan by cons^t, Purkins present.
Between sd Boughan and Thos Broocks Jacob Shearwood and Jonathan Radford Broocks and Shearwood by consent Radford and Broocks present.
Between John Farguson and John Smith, Farguson and Samuel Croxton, Croxton and Francis Boughan, by consent each partie present.
And between Thomas Roane Keziah Brown by Consent.
        J Edmondson
        James Banks
        James Boughan

In pursuance to an order of Vestry held the 9th day of July 1759 in South Farnham Parish we the subscribers have proceeded according to order as followeth (viz)

The line between James Booker and William Fretwell not procession'd Both parties did not appear. The line between Capt John Latane and Joseph Reeves not procession'd the parties did not appear. The other lands in our precinct peaceably procession'd in presence of witnesses. Given under our hands &c. Samuel Allen
        William Cox
        Ambrose Wright

In obedience to an order of Vestry dated the 9th day of July 1759 We the Subscribers Ambrose Jones Thomas Games and Charles Brey have processioned the land within our precinct from Hardys Ferry to Piscataway Ferry down each creek to the River and do make our Return as followeth

Decr ye 12: The line between M^r. John Clements and M^r. James Edmondson peaceably processioned both parties present.

ye 13th The line between Man Page Esqr. and M^c. John Clements is peaceably processioned present Benjamin Jones. The line between Man

Page Esqr and Thomas Games preaceably processioned present Benjamin Jones & Robert Jones.

ye 20th: The line between Man Page Esqr and M^{rs}. Mary Young peaceably processioned present Benj^a Jones and Richard Cauthorn. The line between Man Page Esqr and Charles Brey peaceably processioned present Benj^a Jones overseer. The line between Man Page Esqr and Robert Sp Coleman not processioned Mr Coleman being abset.

          Ambrose Jones
          Thomas Games
          Charles his X mark Brey

[79] [1759 Processioning]
In obedience to an order of vestry bearing date ye 9th day of July 1759 We being appointed to procession the persons lands in the precinct mentioned within the sd order have quietly and peaceably within the time mentioned processioned the same where the people met us. Given under our hands this 21st of April 1760.

          Thomas Burk
          Jos: Burnett

In pursuance to an order of Vestry held for South Farnham Parish the ninth day of July 1759 We the subscribers have peaceably processioned the lands in our precincts according to order afores^d excepting the line between Robt. Sp Coleman and Peter Kemp for lack of Colemans appearance also the line between the s^d Coleman and Joseph Burnett not processioned for lack of the s^d Burnetts appearance. Given under our hands etc.

          James Allen
          Henry Kidd
          Ambrose Gatewood

In pursuance to an order of Vestry held for South Farnham Parish on ye 9th day of July 1759 We the subscribers have proceeded according to the s^d order and processioned all the lands in our precinct peaceably in the presents of Benjamin Waggener & Thomas Waring. Given under our hands this 23^d day Apr^l 1760.

Benj^a Allen
Wm Edmondson

****

[80]   [1763 Processioning]
At a Vestry held for the Parish of South Farnham at Capt James Webbs Piscataway Ferry on the 4th day of Augst 1763.

Present John Upshaw & William Young Church Wardens

Pursuant to an order of Court for the County of Essex bearing date the 18th day of July Anno Dom. one thousand seven hundred sixty and three [1763] whereby it is ordered that the Vestry of each parish within the said county divide their parishes into so many precincts as to them shall seem most convenient for procession[ing] every particular persons land in the several parishes and appoint the particular times for processioning, likewise appoint two intelligent honest freeholders at least of every precinct to see such processioning performed and take and return to the Vestry an account of every persons land they shall procession and of the persons present at the same and what land in their precincts they shall fail to procession and of the particular reasons of such failure.

1st This present Vestry do therefore divide the Parish of South Farnham into twenty precincts and it is ordered that Thos. Clark, Richard Street and Josiah Mctire or any two procession every persons land in their precinct begining at the lower end of Essex County and running to the Gleab Creek from thence to M^r. Leonard Hills Quarter on the Dragon begining the 10th day of Novr. and to finish by the 10th day of Decr. and to make their return as the law directs.

2nd Ordered that Thom^s Wale [Hale?], James Medley Jr and Joshua Boughton or any two procession every persons land in their precinct begining at M^r. Leonard Hills Quarter on the Dragon from thence to Joshua Boughtons and so to the Dragon and from thence to M^{rs}. Adamses Quarter on the River Side begining the fifteenth day of Novr. and to finish by the last day of the same month and to make their return as the law directs.

3rd Ordered that Thomas Newbill, William Bonds, and Andrew Allen or any two procession every persons land in their precinct begining at Joshua Boughtons from thence to Cap.t James Kidds Quarter on the Old Mill Swamp that leads to Piscataway Creek from thence to William Cheneys on the Dragon begining the twentieth day of Nov.r and to finish by the twentieth day of Dec.r and to make their return as the law directs.

4th Ordered that Greensby Evans, Micajah Evans and John Broocke or any two procession every persons land in their precinct begining at M.rs Adams Quarter on the River Side from thence Tylers Creek by John Youngs and so to the Back Road by Thomas Cauthorne from thence down the s.d Road to Joshua Boughtons begining the twenty second day of Nov.r and to finish by the twenty second day of Dec.r and to make their return as the law directs.

5th Ordered that Richard Jeffries, William Mitchel and Henry Cauthorn or any two procession every persons land in their precinct begining at Coll. Robinsons Quarter land by Thomas Cauthorn from thence to Capt. James Webbs Quarter land on the Old Mill Swamp thence down the said Swamp to Piscataway Ferry so down the Main Road to Coll. Robinsons old field begining the twenty sixth day of Nov.r and to finish by the twenty sixth day of Dec.r and to make their return as the law directs.

6th Ordered that John Richards, Smith Young and James Jones or any two procession every persons land in their precinct begining at Coll Robinsons Quarter land by Thomas Cauthorn from thence to the creek where John Philips once lived and all the land between the River and the Road to Piscataway Creek begining the twenty eighth day of Nov.r and to finish by the first day of January and to make their return as the law directs.

[81]   [1763 Processioning]
7th   Ordered that Francis Brezendine John Brezendine and Drury Dobbins or any two of them procession every persons lands in their precinct begining at William Cheynies on the Dragon from thence to the head of Covingtons Mill Swamp and down the Swamp to Coll.o Taylors Quart.r landing from thence up the Road by Thos Williamsons to William

Cheyneys begining the third day of Decr and to finish by the twelfth day of Jany and to make their return as the law directs.

8th Ordered that Philip Kid, William Gordon and William Fletcher or any two procession every persons land in their precinct begining at Capt. Benj^a Smiths Landing and so up Piscataway Creek to the Old Mill from thence along the road to Capt. James Webbs Ordinary from thence down the branch to the Dragon and to William Cheneys from thence to Capt Benj^a Smiths landing begining the fifth day of Decr. and to finish by the fifteenth day of Jany. and to make their return as the law directs.

9th Ordered that Thomas Dunn, Thomas Dennet and Richd Brown or any two procession every persons land in their precinct begining at Mathews Bridge from thence to the Road and down the Road to Elliots old field from thence to the head of the Dragon and down the Dragon to a branch below James Finnies from thence up the s^d branch to Capt. James Webbs Ordinary and along the Road to Mathews Bridge begining the tenth day of Decr. and to finish by the last day of Jany. and to make their return as the law directs.

10th Ordered that Rhodes Greenwood, William Greenwood and George Newbill or any two procession every persons land in their precinct between the two branches of the Dragon from thence up to the Main Road that divideth Essex County from King & Queen County begining the twelfth day of Decr. and to finish by the last day of Jany and to make their return as the law directs.

11th Ordered that John Edmondson, James Banks, and James Booker or any two procession every persons land in their precinct begining at Hales Bridge from thence down the Road to the Long Reach Road from thence to the head of Fishers Mill Swamp and down the Swamp to Mathews Bridge from thence along the Road to the Old Mill from thence up the Swamp to Hales Bridge begining the tenth day of Novr. and to finish by the tenth day of Decr. and to make their return as the law directs.

12th Ordered that Samuel Allen, Ambrose Wright and Henry Cox or any two procession every persons land in their precinct begining at Hales Bridge from thence to the Long Reach Road from thence up the Road to the dividing line of the county from thence to the head of Piscataway

Swamp and down the Swamp to Hales Bridge begining the fifteenth day of Novr. and to finish by the fifteenth day of Decr. and to make their return as the law directs.

13th Ordered that Ambrose Jones, Thomas Games and Charles Brey or any two procession every persons land in their precinct begining at Hardees Ferry on Hoskins Creek from thence to Piscataway Ferry and so down each creek of the River begining the twentieth day of Novr. and to finish by the twentieth day of Decr. and to make their return as the law directs.

14th Ordered that Joseph Burnett John Burnet Ju^r and Augustine Smith or any two procession every persons lands in their precinct between the Little Ferry on Hoskins Creek and Piscataway Ferry and up to Boughans Mill and up to Whites Run Bridge begining the twenty second day of Novr to finish by the twenty second day of Decr and to make their return as the law directs.

[82] [1763 Processioning]
15th Ordered that Richard Thomas Hale Henry Kidd and Ambrose Gatewood or any two procession every persons lands in their precinct between Boughans Mill and across to Warings Old Mill and up to Hales Bridge and across to Warings sd Old Mill Swamp begining the twenty sixth day of Nov^r & to finish by the twenty sixth day of Dec and to make their retur[n] as the law directs.

16th Ordered that Capt. John Latane, James Pamplin and Jonathan Shearwood procession every persons land in their precinct between Hales Bridge and Warings Old Mill Swamp and up to the dividing line of Essex County from King & Queen County begining the twenty eighth day of Novr. and to finish by the first day of January and to make their return as the law directs.

17th Ordered that William Porter, Reuben Waganer and William Edmondson or any two procession every persons land in the Mill Neck from John Armstrongs across to William Greenhills begining the third day of Decr. and to finish by the twelfth day of Jany. and to make their return as the law directs.

18th Ordered that John Fantleroy Gen^t, Benj^a. Allen & Benj^a. Waggener or any two procession every persons lands in their precinct between John Armstrongs and William Greenhills on Col. Warings Mill and so across to Henry Tandys begining the fifth day of Decr. and to finish by the fifteenth day of January and to make their return as the law directs.

19th Ordered that John Hill, Edmond Pagett and William Webb or any two procession every persons lands in their precinct between Col. Warings Mill and Henry Tandys and up to Charles Wallers from thence to M^r. James Rennolds begining the tenth day of Decr. and to finish by the last day of January and to make their return as the law directs.

20th Ordered that Leonard Hill, William Watkins and Rich^d. Hill Junr or any two procession every persons lands in the upper precinct to King & Queen begining the twelfth day of Decr. to finish the last day of January and to make their return as the law directs.

     Signed
     John Upshaw ⎫
     William Young ⎬ Church Wardens
Truly Registered p^r. Henry Vass Clk of the Vestry

    ****

At a Vestry held for South Farnham Parish at Mr. William Degge's Piscataway Ferry on the 9th day of Octob^r. 1764.
  Present
  John Upshaw ⎫
  Samuel Peachey ⎬ Church Wardens

James Webb, John Clements, Thomas Roane, William Mountague, William Young, and Archibald Ritchie Gent^m.

It is ordered that the returns made by the processioners be truly registered in the Vestry Book appointed for that purpose and that they be Exam^d over by the Vestry to see that they be rightly entered within six months after ye date hereof.   John Upshaw
              Samuel Peachey

[83]   [1763 Processioning]
Pursuant to an order of the Vestry of South Farnham Parrish dated the 4th day of August 1763 We the subscribers have procession'd the several lines in the Lower precinct as followeth Viz^t.

The line between Titus Farguson and Thomas Taff present the sd Taff.
The line between Capt Wm Montague and Thomas Taff present the said Taff.
The line between Augustine Owen and Thomas Taff present the s^d Taff & s^d Owen.
The line between Rice Jones and Samuel Mountague present the s^d Jones & Wm Owen.
The line between Rice Jones and John Cloudas present Augustine Owen.
The line between Rice Jones and Capt. Mountague present the said Jones.
Part of the line between Susanna Parker and John Cloudas the other part not to be found present Abner Cloudas.
The line between Susanna Parker and Capt. Wm Mountague present the s^d Mountague Robt Clark and Josiah Mctier.
The line between John Bush and Capt Wm Mountague present the s^d Bush Robt Clark and the s^d Mountague.
The line between Capt Wm Mountague and Titus Farguson present the s^d Mountague Robt Clark and s^d Farguson.
The lines between Titus Farguson and John Bush present the s^d Bush.
The line between Joseph Minter and Susanna Parker present John Bush.
The line between Jo. Minter and Thomas Watts present John Bush.
The line between Thomas Watt and John Bush present Jo. Minter.
The line between Capt Wm Mountague and John Bush present John Bush and Joseph Minter.
The line between Capt Mountague and Robt Clark present Rice Jones and Samuel Mountague.
John Sadlars line present Chatten Charles.
The line between John Sadlar and Josiah Mctier present John Cornelius.
The line between Josiah Mctier and Richard Street present John Cornelius.
The line between Josiah Macktier and Thomas Clark present Henry Street.
The line between Thomas Clark and Reuben Shelton present the s^d Shelton and Henry Street.
The line between Henry Street and Josiah Mctier present the s^d Street and

John Sadlar.
The line between Henry Street and Reuben Shelton present the sd Street John Sadlar and s^d Shelton.
The line between Henry Street and Abraham Mountague present the s^d Street and John Sadlar.
The line between Abraham Mountague and Thomas Clark present John Sadlar and Henry Street.
The line between Abraham Mountague and Richard Street present Henry Street and John Sadlar.
The line between Thomas Clark and Richard Street present John Sadlar and Henry Street.
The line between John Sadlar and Richard Street present Reuben Shelton and John Cornelius.
The line between Abraham Mountague and Josiah Mctier present Henry Street and John Sadlar.
The line between Capt Wm Mountague and Thomas Watts present Wm Amiss and Philip Patterson.
The line between Wm Amiss and Thomas Watts present Thomas Carlton and s^d Amiss.
The line between Samuel Mountague and Wm Amiss present Philip Patterson and s^d Amiss.
The line between William Amiss and Leonard Hill's orphans present Philip Patterson and sd Amiss and Thomas Carlton.

Thomas Clark
Richard Street

[84]   [1763 Processioning]
1763

In obedience to an order of Vestry we the Subscribers have processioned the lands within our precinct as followeth

Processioned the line between Leonard Hill dec^d orphans and Ja^s Medley Junr Thomas Carlton and Thos Hunley present. Also the line between Mr John Beale and Ja^s Medley Junr, Thomas Carlton and Thos Hunley present. The line between John Smith dec^d orphans and Ja^s Medley, Thos Carlton and Thos Hunley present. The line between John Smith decd orphans and Robert Hunley, Nenn Miskell and Robert Hunley present. The line between Leonard Hill decd orphans and Robert Hunley, Thos

Carlton and Robert Hunley present. The line between John Smith dec^d orphans and Charles Sanders dec^d orphan, Samuel Smith present. The line between John Smith dec^d orphans and Samuel Smith, s^d S. Smith present. The line between Samuel Smith & Charles Sanders dec^d orphan, s^d Samuel Smith present. The line between Samuel Smith and John Boughton, party's present.

The line between John Boughton and Henry Vass, John Boughton present.
The line between John Boughton and Charles Sanders dec^{yd} Orphan, John Boughton present.
The line between Samuel Smith and Alex. S. Sanders, partys present.
The line between Ja^s Medley and Robert Hunley, party's present.
The line between Thos Watts and Ja^s. Medley, partys present. The line between Maj^r. Shackelford and Thos. Watts, Peter Broocke and Wm Broocke present.
The line between Thos Watts and Gleeb, Wm Watts present.
The line between Majr Shackelford and Mr John Beale, Peter Broocke Wm Broocke present.
The line between Col. Corban and Mr John Beale, Peter Broocke present.
The line between Col. Corban and Mr Richd Adm^s, Peter Broocke present.
The line between Mr. John Beale and Henry Vass, James Medley Senr. present.
The line between s^d Beale and James Medley Senr, s^d Medley Senr present.
The line between Ja^s. Medley Senr. and Charles Sanders Dec^d Orphans s^d Medley present.
The line between John Boughton and Birds orphans, John Boughton present.
The line between Joshua Boughton and Alex. S. Sanders, John Boughton Junr. present.
The line between M^r. Richd Adm^s and M^r. John Beale's back land is not to be found also the line between Adm^s and Henry Vass not to be found also the line between Henry Vass and Charles Sanders Dec^d. orphans not to be found.

Given under our hands   James Medley Junr
Thomas Watts
Joshua Boughton

In obedience to an order of Vestry made on the 4th day of August 1763 We the Subscribers hath procession'd the lines as followeth

Novr. 24th The line between M^r. Adames and George Bird procession'd. The line between M^r. Adams and George Russell procession'd. The line between Mr. Adams and William Mountague procession'd. The line between George Bird Gen^t. and William Mountague procession'd. The line between Joshua Boughton Wm Broocke & George Newbill procesion'd.

Novr 25th The line between Samuel Broocke and Isaac Williams procession'd. The line between Samuel Broocke and John Broocke procession'd. The line between Samuel Broocke and the heirs of John Philips. Processioned the line between Samuel Broocke and the heirs of John Evans jr procession'd. The line between John Broocke and Henry Gardner procession'd. The line between Henry Gardner and Samuel Broocke procession'd. The line between Henry Gardner and the heirs of John Evans procession'd, also another Line between Henry Gardner and the above said heirs from the Main Road up the Lowest Bottom to Beals old line through the old field procession'd peaceably.

[85]   [1763 Processioning]
The line between the Heirs of John Evans and John Mitchel quietly and peaceably by both parties procession'd. The line between the Heirs of John Evans and Greensbe Evans procession'd. The line between the above Heirs and John Dunn procession'd.

Novr 26th The line between Samuel Peachey Gent and Greensbe Evans procession'd. Between the said Peachey's land and an old Mill dam known by the name of Hudsons Old Mill Dam procession'd. The line between Samuel Peachey Gen^t and George Russell procession'd. The line between the above Peachey and the Heirs of John Philips procession'd. The line between Samuel Peachey Gent and Heirs of Leonard Hill procession'd. The line between John Webb and Greensbe Evans procession'd. That is to say a NW course between the above John and Greensbe. The line between John Webb and Micajah Evans procession'd. The line between John Webb and John Young procession'd.

Novr 27th The line between John Mitchel and Mary Young procession'd. The line between John Mitchel and Greensbe Evans procession'd. The line between Greensbe Evans and Micajah Evans procession'd. The line between William Mountague and George Russell not procession'd they both agreeing to settle the dispute themselves.

Decr 22 The lines between John Dunn and Greensbe Evans not procession'd. The sd Dunn not being at home the day appointed.
                        Greensbe Evans
                        John Brook

Pursuant to an order of Vestry of South Farnham Parish bearing date the 4th day of August 1763 We the subscribers have procession'd the lands in our in our precinct as follow Viz^t

The line between Biroms orphans & William Fletcher in the presence of John Birom and William Fletcher.
The line between Wm Fletcher & Thomas Williamson in presence of Wm Fletcher & John Birom.
The line between Thomas Cox Sner and Thomas Cox Jr in presence of Thomas Cox Senr.
The line between Thomas Cox Senr and Joseph Mann in presence of John Mann and Thomas Cox.
The line between Thomas Cox and Thomas Williamson in presence of Thomas Cox and Philip Kid.
The line between Thomas Cox and Philip Kid in presence of Thomas Cox and Philip Kid.
The line between Joseph Mann and Philip Kid in presence of John Mann and Philip Kid.
The line between Constant Edmondson and John Rodden in presence of John Rodden and John Mann.
The line between Constant Edmondson and William Fletcher in presence of William Fletcher and John Mann.
The line between Mary Brook and Constant Edmondson in presence of Mary Brooke and John Mann.
The line between Constant Edmondson and James Edmondson in presence of John Mann and Philip Kid.
The line between John Rodden and Philip Kid in presence of John

Rodden and Philip Kid.
The line between Philip Kid and Thomas Williamson in presence of John Williamson jr and Philip Kid.
The line between William Gordon and Thomas Williamson in presence of John Williamson jr and Philip Kid.
The line between William Gordon and John Davis in presence of Davis and Philip Kid.

[86]   [1763 Processioning]
The line between John Davis and Isaac Jordan in presence of John Davis and Philip Kid.
The line between John Davis and John Rodden in presence of the parties.
The line between John Davis and Evan Davis in presence of the parties.
The line between Philip Kid and Evan Davis in presence of the parties.
The line between Evan Davis and James Webb in presence of the parties.
The line between Thoms Williamson and James Webb in the presence of Thomas Williamson.
The line between Nathan Breedlove and Trebles orphans in the presence of Nathan Breedlove.
The line between Joseph Mann and Trebles orphans in the presence of Nathan Breedlove.
The line between Joseph Mann and Nathan Breedlove in the presence of Nathan Breedlove.
The line between Joseph Mann and Thomas Bush of presence of Robert Mann and Thomas Bush.
The line between John Oneal and Joseph Mann in presence of Robert Mann and William Johnson.
The line between John Oneal and Peter Treble in presence of William Johnson.
The line between Joseph Mann and Peter Treble in presence of Robert Mann.
The line between Peter Treble and Thomas Cole in presence of William Collens and William Johnson.
The line between Thomas Cole and Nathan Breedlove in presence of Nathan Breedlove and William Collens.
The line between Nathan Breedlove and Joseph Mann in presence of Robert Mann.
The line between Francis Jones and Allaman Breedlove in presence of the

parties.
The line between Francis Jones and Trebles Orphans in presence of Francis Jones and Nathan Breedlove.
The line between William Williamson and Mary Brooke in presence of Francis Jones.
The line between Francis Brizindine and William Cheney is presence of the parties.
The line between Francis Brizindine and Thomas Cox in presence of Francis Brizidine and William Cheney.
The line between Francis Brizidine [&] Thomas Bush in presence of the parties.
The line between Francis Brizidine and John Oneal in presence of the parties.
The line between Thomas Bush and John Oneal in presence the parties.
The line between Thomas Bush and Robert James in the presence of Thomas Bush.
The line between Thomas Bush and John Vass in presence of Thomas Bush.
The line between Robert James and John Vass in presence of John Vass j^r and Thomas Bush.
The line between John Vass and Richard Johnson in presence of John Vass j^r and Thomas Bush.

          Francis Brizindine
          John Brizindine

[87] [1763 Processioning]
Pursuant to an order of Vestry of South Farnham Parish bearing date the 4th day of August 1763 We the subscribers have processioned the lands in our precinct as follow Vizt

The line between John Brizendine and Thomas Cox in presence of the parties.
The line between Thomas Cox and Robert Akers in presence of the parties.
The line between Robert Akers and Elizabeth Cooper in presence of Robert Akers and Thomas Cox.
The line between John Oneal and John Williamson in presence of the

parties.
The line between John Williamson and John Davis in presence of the parties.
The line between John Davis and Isaac Jordon in presence of Thomas Cox and John Davis.
The line between James Webb and John Williamson in presence of John Williamson and John Davis.
The line between James Webb and John Davis in presence of John Davis and Thomas Cox.
The line between Isaac Jordon and John Hays in present of Thomas Cox and John Hays.
The line between John Hays and James Turner in prsence of John Hays and Thomas Cox.
The line between Isaac Williamson and Thomas Turner in presence of the parties.
The line between Thomas Turner and William Gordon in presence of the parties.
The line between Thomas Williamson and Isaac Williamson in presence of Isaac Williamson and Richard Williamson.
The line between Thomas Williamson and William Gordon in presence of William Gordon and Richard Williamson.
The line between William Gordon and Isaac Williamson in presence of the parties.
The line between Leroy Hipkins and John Good in presence of the parties.
The line between John Good and Thomas Williamson in presence of Leroy Hipkins and John Good.
The line between Isaac Williamson and Leroy Hipkins in presence of Leroy Hipkins and Richard Williamson.
The line between Leroy Hipkins and James Turner in presence of Leroy Hipkins and Thomas Turner.
The line between James Turner and Berry Taylor in presence of Thomas Turner.
The line between Leroy Hipkins and William Dunn in presence of the parties.
The line between John Clements and William Ramsey in presence of William Ramsey.
The line between Wm Ramsey and Wm Snodgrass in presence of Wm Ramsey and Leroy Hipkins.

The line between John Tylers orphans and Leroy Hipkins in presence of Arthur Tate and Leroy Hipkins.
The line between Leroy Hipkins and Wm Ramsey in presence of the parties.

>Philip Kidd
>William Gordon
>William Fletcher

[88]   [1763 Processioning]
Pursuant to an order of Vestry bearing date the 4th day of August 1763 We the subscribers have processioned the lands in our precinct as follows (Viz)
The line between Richard Brown and James Turner in the presence of Richard Brown and Wm Dunn Junr.
The line between James Webb and Richard Brown in the presence of James Webb and Richard Brown.
The line between James Webb and Thomas Dunn in the presence of James Webb and Thomas Dunn.
The line between James Webb and John Dickerson in the presence of James Webb and John Dickerson.
The line between Thoms Henry Broocke and Thomas Dunn in the presence of the parties.
The line between John Williamson and Thomas Henry Broocke in the presence of both parties.
The line between John Williamson and Eliz^a Allen in the presence of John Williamson and Henry Dunn.
The line between Benjamin Dunn and Susanna Crow in the presence of Benj^a Dunn and John Crow.
The line between Susanna Crow and Eliz^a Allen in the presence of John Crow and Henry Dunn.
The line between Jane Baker and Eliz^a Allen in the presence of Henry Dunn.
The line of Eliz^a Allen and Thomas Miller in the presence of Henry Dunn.
The line between John Dickerson and Luke Covington in the presence of Agrippa Dunn.
The line between James Webb and Luke Covington in the presence of

James Webb and Agrippa Dunn. The line between Drury Dobbins and John Brizindine in the presence of James Webb and the parties. The line between James Webb and Drury Dobbins in the presence of both parties. The line between James Webb and John Williamson in the presence of both the parties. The line between Thomas Dennett and William Dunn Jun[r] in the presence of the parties. Ended the 22 day of January 1764.

        Thomas Dunn
        Thomas Dennett
        Richard Brown

Pursuant to the order of Vestry dated -- 1763 We the Subscribers have processioned the land in our precincts as followeth Viz

The line dividing between Thomas Dunn John Edmondson Wm Dunn & Nathaniel Dunn procession'd by consent in presence of the proprietors. The line between Daniel Hodghill, John Fargeson and John Smith procession'd by consent of each partie. The Line between Fargeson John Croxton Sam[l] Croxton & Fran[s] Boughan procession'd in their presence & by consent. The line between Cap[t]. Thomas Roane Jacob Shearwood & Doc[tr] Clements procession'd by consent in prsence of the sd Roane & Shearwood.

    pr   J Edmondson
          James Booker

PS As also y[e] line between John Boughan and Henry Purkins procession'd in their presence.

Pursuant to an order of the Vestry of South Farnham Parish We the Subscribers have peaceably procession'd and mark'd the line of all persons lands in our precinct that was found or shewn to us between John Armstrongs and Wm Greenhills and Coll. Warings Old Mill and so on to Henry Tandies line. In presence of Coll. Francis Waring Mr John Rennolds and Robert Paine Waring Robert White and Nathan Waggener.

Given under our hands this eighteenth day of January 1764.
        Benj[a] Allen
        Benj[a] Waggener

****

[89]   [1771 Processioning]
At a vestry held for South Farnham Parish at Capt James Edmondsons Piscataway Ferry on the 8th day of Octob^r 1771

Present
The Revd Alex^r Cruden Clk
William Montague and William Roane, Church Wardens
John Upshaw Thomas Roane Arch^d Ritchie Saml Peachey John Richards James Campbell James Webb, Meriw^r Smith, and William Young Gent^m.

Pursuant to an order of Court for the County of Essex bearing date September Court Anno dom^y one thousand seven hundred seventy and one [1771] whereby it is ordered that the Vestry of each parish within the said county divide their parishes into so many precincts as to them shall seem most convenient for processioning every particular persons land in the several parishes and appoint the particular times for processioning, likewise appoint two intelligent honest freeholders at least of every precinct to see such processioning performed and take and return to the Vestry an account of every persons land they shall procession and of the persons present at the same and what land in their precincts they shall fail to procession and of the particular reasons of such failure.

This present Vestry do therefore divide the Parish of South Farnham into nineteen precincts and it is ordered that Robert Clark, Richard Street and William Brooke Junr or any two procession every persons land in their precinct begining at the lower end of the County and running at the Glebe Creek from thence to M^r. Leonard Hills Quarter on the Dragon begining the tenth day of November and to finish by the tenth day of December and to make their return as the law directs.

2^d Ordered that Abr^m. Saunders, James Medley Junr. and Robert Hundley or any two procession every persons land in their precinct begining at M^r. Leonard Hills Quarter on the Dragon from thence to Joshua Boughtons and so to the Dragon and from thence to M^{rs}. Adams's Quarter on the River Side begining the fifteenth day of Novem^r and to finish by the last day of the same month and to make their return as the law directs.

3rd Ordered that Thomas Newbill, William Bond and Andrew Allen or any two procession every persons land in their precinct begining at Joshua Boughtons from thence to Capt. James Wells Quarter on the Old Mill Swamp that leads to Piscataway Creek from thence to William Cheneys on the Dragon begining the twentyeth day of November and to finish by the twentyeth day of Decemb^r and to make their return as the law directs.

4th Ordered that Richard Philips, John Broocke & Henry Gardner or any two procession every persons land in their precinct from M^{rs}. Adams to Gatewoods Creek by Henry Youngs thence up the Creek to the Main Road by M^{rs}. Mary Youngs so along the Road down to Joshua Boughton begining the twenty second day of November and to finish by the twenty second day of December and to make their return as the law directs.

5th Ordered that Richard Jeffries Richard Fuller and Henry Cauthorn or any two procession every persons land in their precinct from William Gatewoods land near M^{rs}. Mary Young from thence to Capt James Webbs Quarter by his Mill thence along the Swamp to Piscataway Creek and down the Creek to the Ferry thence down the Raod to the begining begining the twenty sixth day of November & to finish by the twenty sixth day of December and to make their return as the law directs.

6th Ordered that William Gatewood Junr James Jones & Thomas Cauthorn or any two procession every persons land in their precinct from Wm Gatewood Land near M^{rs}. Mary Youngs from thence to the Creek by Richard Philips's so down the creek thence including all the lands between the Main Road & the River to Piscataway Creek begining the twenty eight day of November & to finish by the first day of January and to make their return as the law directs.

[90]   [1771 Processioning]
7th Ordered that Francis Brizendine John Brizendine and John Dobbyns or any two procession every persons land in their precinct begining at William [Cheney] on the Dragon from thence to the head of Covingtons Mill Swamp and down the Swamp to Mrs. Eliza Wrights landing from thence up the Road by Thos Williamsons to William Cheyneys begining [the] third day of December and to finish by the twelfth day of January and to make their return as the law directs.

8th Ordered that Philip Kidd, Thomas Gordon and Isaac Jordan or any two procession every persons land in their precinct begining at Mrs. Eliz^a Wrights landing and so up Piscataway Creek to the Old Mill from thence along the Road to Mr. James Webbs Ordinary from thence down the branch to the Dragon and to William Cheneys from thence to M^{rs}. Eliz^a Wrights Landing begining the fifth day of Decemb^r and to finish by the fifteenth day of January and to make their return as the law directs.

9th Ordered that William Dunn (white), Thomas Dennet and Richard Brown or any two procession every persons land in their precinct begining at Mathews Bridge from thence to the Road and down the Road to Elliots old field from thence to the head of the Dragon and down the Dragon to a branch below John Webb Junr from thence up the s^d branch to Mr Webbs Ordinary and along the Road to Mathews Bridge begining the tenth day of Decr and to finish by the last day of January and to make their returns as the law directs.

10th Ordered that John Cheney, James Greenwood & William Greenwood or any two procession every persons land in their precinct begining between the two branches of the Dragon from thence up the Main Road that divideth Essex County from King & Queen County begining the twelfth day of Decr. and to finish by the last day of January and to make their return as the law directs.

11th Ordered that William Dunn (Black), James Booker & James Banks or any two procession every persons land in their precinct begining at Hales Bridge from thence down the Road to the Long Reach Road from thence to the head of Fishers Mill Swamp and down the Swamp to Mathews Bridge from thence along the Road to the Old Mill from thence up the Swamp to Hales Bridge begining the tenth day of Novr. and to finish by the tenth day of Decem^r. and to make their return as the law directs.

12th Ordered that Samuel Allen, Joseph Ryland and Richard Holt Junr or any two procession every persons land in their precinct begining at Hales Bridge from thence to the Long Reach Road from thence up the Road to the dividing line of the County from thence to the head of Piscataway Swamp and down the Swamp to Hales Bridge begining the fifteenth day of Novr. and to finish by the fifteenth day of Decem^r. and to make their return as the law directs.

13th Ordered that John Edmondson Junr, Charles Bray and Thomas Games or any two procession every persons land in their precinct begining at Hoskins Bridge from thence to Piscataway Ferry and so down each branch to the River begining the twentieth day of Novr. and to finish by the twentieth day of Decr. and to make their return as the law directs.

14th Ordered that Pitman [Tilman?] Clements, John Burnet and Richard Burk or any two procession every persons land in their precinct between Hoskins branch and Piscataway Ferry and up to Boughtons Mill and up to Whites Run Bridge begining the twenty second day of Novr. and to finish by the twenty second day of Decr. and to make their return as the law directs.

15th Ordered that Richard Thomas Haile Henry Kidd and Thomas Allen or any two procession every persons land in their precinct between Boughans Mill and across to Warings Mill and to Hailes Bridge and across to Warings Mill Swamp begining the twenty sixth day of Novr and to finish by the twenty sixth day of Decr and to make their return as the law directs.

[91]   [1771 Processioning]
16th Ordered the Col^o John Latane Thomas Dix and Cheyney Gatewood or any two procession every persons land in their precinct between Hailes Bridge and Warings Old Mill Swamp and up to the dividing line of Essex County from King & Queen County begining the twenty sixth day of Novr and to finish by the first day of January and to make their return as the law directs.

17th Ordered that Abra^m. Smith, Andrew Crawford and William Edmondson or any two procession every persons land in the Mill Neck from Abra^m. Smiths across to Fauntleroys late dwelling plantation begining the third day of Decr. and to finish by the twelfth day of January and to make their return as the law directs.

18th Ordered that Robert Payne Waring, John Smith and Nathan

Waggener or any two procession every persons land in their precinct from Smiths and Fauntleroys to Waring Old Mill from thence across to Capt. William Roanes land fomerly Tandy's begining the fifth day of Decr. and to finish by the fifteenth day of January and to make their return as the law directs.

19th Ordered that Thomas Sthreshley, William Webb and Erasmus Jones or any two procession every persons land in their precinct from Warings Old Mill and Roans land formerly Tandy's to the upper end of the parish begining the tenth day of Decr. and to finish by the last day of January and to make their return as the law directs.

William Roane Ch Warden

Truly Registered p^r. Henry Vass Clk of the Vestry

[92]   [1771 Processioning]
1st [precinct] Pursuant to an order of Vestry bearing date the 8th day of Octob^r Wee the Subscribers have processioned the several lines in the lower precinct of South Farnham Parish in Essex County as followeth (viz)

The line between Abraham Mountague & Henry Street, present John Sadler.
The line between Abraham Mountague & Josiah McTire, present John Sadler.
The line between Abraham Mountague & Titus Ferguson, present John Sadler.
The line between Richard Street & Titus Farguson, present John Sadler.
The line between Abraham Mountague & Richard Street, present John Sadler.
The line between Josiah McTyre & Titus Farguson, present John Sadler.
The line between Henry Street & Josiah McTyre, present John Sadler.
The line between Richard Street and John Sadler.
The line between Titus Farguson and Reubin Bush.
The line between Titus Farguson and Elizabeth Bush.
The line between Capt. W^m. Montague and Elizabeth Bush.

The line between Capt. W^m. Montague and Titus Farguson.
The line between John Cloudas & Thomas Taff, present John Cloudas.
The line between John Cloudas & John Owen, present Thomas Taff.
The line between John Owen & Thomas Taff, present John Cloudas.
The line between John Cloudas & Rice Jones Orphans estate.
The line between the orphan of Leonard Hill & W^m. Broocke, present Peter Broocke.
The line between W^m. Broocke & Mary Watts, pres^t Peter Broocke.
The line between W^m. Broocke & Samuel Montague, Pst Chating Charles.
The line between Capt. W^m. Montague and Mary Watts.
The line between Mary Watts & Reuben Bush, present Thomas Dean.
The line between Reubin Bush and Thomas Dean.
The line between Capt. W^m. Montague & Reubin Bush, present Thomas Dean.
The line between Henry Armistead and Thomas Dean.
The line between Capt. W^m. Montague & the orphan of Rice Jones.
The line begween Capt. W^m. Montague and Henry Armistead.
The line between Joseph Minter and Thomas Dean.
The line between Capt. Wm Montague & Samuel Montague, present. George Blackley & John Montague & the said Samuel Montague.
The line between Robert Clark & Capt. W^m. Montague.
          Robert Clarke
          William Broocke

2^d In obedience to any order of Vestry dated the 8th of Octob^r 1771 Wee the Subscribers have processioned the lines in our precinct Viz

Begining at the line between Leonard Hill & Robert Hunley by consent of Mr James Campbell present Robert Hunley and James Fisher.
The line between the s^d Hills land & James Medley Junr, present Mr Medley & James Fisher.
Also the line between Robert Hunley & James Medley Junr, the parties present & James Fisher.
The line between Robert Hunley & Orphans of John Smith dec^d by consent of Capt James Webb, present Robert Hunley and James Fisher.

[93] [1771 Processioning]
The line of the said orphans land & Samuel Smith by consent of Capt

Webb, present Laurence Smith & Chatten Charles.
The line between James Medley Junr & Charles Saunders, parties present.
The line between John Beale & Henry Vass, parties present.
The line between said Beale & James Medley Junr, parties present.
The line between Richard Adams & John Beales River side tract not to be found. Also the line between the said Adams and Beale forrest do. [ditto] not to be found.
Processioned the line between Col^o Corbin & M^r. Beal. Corbin had notice but did not attend. Beal present.
The line between Maj^r. Shackleford & John Beal. John Brim present.
The line between John Beal & James Medley Senr, present M^r. Beal & M^r. Vass.
The line between Thomas Watts dec^d land & James Medley Junr, Charles Saunders present.
The line between Shackleford & Watkins Orphans, Charles Saunders present.
The line between the Glebe land & Shackleford prsent Charles Saunders.
The line between the Glebe land & Watts's Orphans, present Charles Saunders.
The line between the lands of Samuel Smith, Charles Saunders, John Boughton, Joshua Boughton & Alexander Saunders by consent of the parties.
Also the dividing line between Samuel Smith & Alex^r. Saunders, present William Dollerson. Also the line between Joshua Boughton and his son Thomas.
The line between Joshua Boughton & John Boughton by consent of the parties. Present Thomas Boughton.
The line between Corbin & Adams, present Christopher Broocke and W^m. Southern.
The line between Richard Adams & Henry Vass not to be found.
The line between John Boughton & Henry Vass not to be found.
   Decemb^r 20th 1771 p^r Alex^r. Saunders
              James Medley Junr.
              Robert Hunley

3^d Pursuant to any order of a Vestry made the 8th day of Octob^r. 1771 We the Subscribers have processiond every mans land in our precinct as followeth

Decemb^r. 4th The line between W^m. Bond & Andrew Allen & W^m. Bomar & Henry Crutcher & Bomar & between Bomar & Crutcher and between Crutcher & John Blatt & between Blatt & Bond in presence of W^m. Bomar & John Blatt.

Then the lines between Newman Brockenbrough & Thomas Newbill & between Reuben Broocke & Brockenbr^h & Hipkins's a line so calld in the possession of Fran^s Smith by the consent of Mr Brockenbrough in the presence of his overseer.

The line between William Broocke & Brockenbrough and the line between Wm Broocke & Henry Crutcher & Thomas Newbill and Crutcher in presence of Henry Crtucher Richard Broocke and Mr Brockenbroughs overseer.

Then the line between Wm Young Junr & Thomas Newbill and between Young & Thomas Broocke present Wm Youngs overseer with Youngs consent.

Then the line between Thomas Broocke & Alex^r Bomar and between Thomas Broocke & John Broocke & between John Broocke & Andrew Allen & between John Broocke & Wm Bomar & Alex^r Bomar in presence of Thos Broocke John Broocke & Wm Bomar & in their presence a line between Thos Broocke & Fran^s Brizendine.

[94]   [1771 Processioning]
The line between Ursula Evans & John Dunn present John Evans.
The line between John Dunn & Cheyneys orphans land, present Jam^s Dunn.
The line between Richard Fuller & said orphans land, between Fuller and Griffing Johnson & Mary Young, present Fuller & Johnson.
The line between W^m. Smith & W^m. Bomar & Alex^r Bomar and W^m. Smith & Henry Gardner in presence of W^m. Smith.

A short line between Cheyneys Orphans land and Philip Cheney and between Capt. Smiths mill land and the said Cheneys and Capt. Smith and John Dunn, in presence of Capt. Smiths overseer and by consent of the others.

Thomas Newbill
Wm Bond
Andrew Allen

4th Pursuant to an order of Vestry bearing date the 8th day of Octob^r 1771 Wee the Subscribers have procession'd every mans lands in our precinct only a line between John Webb and the Orphan of Charles Evans as followeth

Decemb^r. 31st. 1771. Began the line between Richard Adams & George Bird in presence of Christopher Broocke & Geo. Saunders overseers.

Jany 3^d. 1772. the line between Joshua Boughton & John Boughton and between John Boughton & Geo Bird and between Joshua Boughton & W^m. Broocke & Isaac Williams & between William Mountague and Richard Philips & the line between Mountague and Leonard Broocke & between Isaac Williams & Fran^s. Smith In presence of John Boughton & Thos. Boughton & Reuben Broocke & W^m. Mountague.

Jany. 11th. the line between Reuben Broocke & Leo: Broocke & between Leo: Broocke & Ursula Evans & John Dunn & between Henry Gardner & Reuben Broocke & Leo: Broocke & between Dianna Evans, John Dunn & Richard Philips in presence of James Dunn & John Johnson.

Jany. 16th. the line between Samuel Peachey & Russell & round Russels between it & Richard Phillips & between Samuel Peachey and James Campbell & Diana Evans & between Ursula Evans & W^m. Young Junr. in presence of Samuel Peachey, John Evans & Thomas Evans & W^m. Young Junr.

March 30th the line between John Webb & Diana Evans (except the line above mention'd was hindered by John Webb) and round Henry Youngs line & W^m. Gatewoods & Philip Gatewoods in presence of Henry Young & W^m. Gatewood.

Richard Phillips
Henry Gardner

5th Essex P[recin]ct
In obedience to an order of the Vestry of S°. Farnham Parish for that purpose we have processioned the lines of the several persons lands in our precincts as follows (vizt)

Between Griffin Johnson and Richard Jeffries, Richard Fuller & the widow Mitchell, in the presence of sd Johnson and Wm Mitchell.
Between the Widow Mitchell and Richard Jeffries in the presence of the sd Wm Mitchell.
Between the Widow Mitchell and James Webb Gent sd Webb & Thos Johnson in the presence of the sd Wm Mitchell & Webb.
Between Vincent Cauthorn and sd Jeffries, Henry Cauthorn & Jeffires, Henry Cauthorn and Vincent Cauthorn in presence of Vincent Cauthorn.

[95]   [1771 Processioning]
Between John Patterson decd and sd Vincent Cauthorn in presence of sd Cauthorn and John Patterson.
Between said Patterson and Jeffries in presence of the sd John Patterson.
Between said Jeffries and Samuel Piles, Jeffries and James Webb in present of said Piles and John Patterson.
Between the said Samuel Piles and James Webb in Piles's presence.
Between the said Jeffries and William Gatewood.
   November 26th 1771   Richard Jeffries
                  Richard Fuller
                  Henry Cothron

6th   Pursuant to an order of Vestry of South Farnham Parish dated the 8th day of Octobr. 1771 We the subscribers have procession'd the lands mentioned in the sd order as followeth (vizt)

Novr 26th 1771 we processioned the line between John Richards and Wm. Gatewood in presence of each party.
Thence the line between John Richards & Wm Young in presence of Henry Young & by consent of Wm Young.
Thence the line between John Richards & Vincent Cauthorn in presence of the parties, thence the line between John Richards and Thomas Cauthorn in presence of the parties Vincent Cauthorn & Henry Young thence the line between John Richard and James Jones in presence of the

parties and Henry Young.

Novr. 28th 1771. We processioned the line between John Richard and Henry Cauthorn in presence of the parties, thence the line between William Young & Capt. James Webb in presence of the parties, thence the line between Capt. James Webb & Col^o. Meriwether Smith in presence of James [Webb] & W^m. Young by cons^t of Col^o. Smith, thence the line between Wm Young & Arch^d McCall in presence of M^r. Young & by consent of Archibald McCall, thence the line between W^m. Young and Col^o. Meri^r Smith in presence of W^m. Young & by consent of Col^o Smith thence the line between Wm Young and Wm Smith in presence of William Young & by consent of William Smith.

Novr. 30th. 1771. We procession'd the line between W^m. Young & Vincent Cauthorn in presence of Vincent Cauthorn & by consent of Wm Young, thence the line between Vincent Cauthorn and William Smith in presence of Vincent Cauthorn and by consent of Wm Smith, thence the line between Vincent Cauthorn & Thomas Cauthorn in presence of the parties, thence the line between Vincent Cauthorn and James Jones in presence of the parties.

Thence the line between Vincent Cauthorn & Smith Young in presence of Vincent Cauthorn & by consent of Smith Young.

Thence the line between Thomas Cauthorn and James Jones in presence of the parties, thence the line between Col^o Meriwether Smiths dwelling plantation and Archibald McCalls land in presence of the parties and William Smith. Thence the line between Archibald McCalls land and the sd Smiths land called Owens's, in presence of the parties & Wm Smith. In processioning this line we begun at the corner in Youngs line and proceeded thence by marcked tree which we remrcked to a branch runing through sd land called Owens and Mr McCall objected to the line beingmarked from the sd branch to the begining white oak on Piscataway Creek side, thence the line between Arch^d McCall & William Smith in presence of the parties, thence the line between Col^o Meriwether Smith and Wm Wmith in presence of the parties.

Decr 8th We processioned the line between Doc^{tr} Ewen Clements and

Smith Young in presence of Doc^tr Clements & Henry Clements & by consent of Smith Young.

[96]   [1771 Processioning]
Thence the line between Doc^tr Ewen Clements and Wm Smith in presence of Doc^tr Clements & Henry Clements and by consent of Wm Smith, thence the line between Doc^tr Ewen Clements & Col° Meriw^r Smith in presence of the parties, thence the line between Wm Wmith & Smith Young by consent of the parties. Given under our hands.
William Gatewood
James Jones
Thomas Cauthorn

7th   Pursuant to an order of a Vestry made Octob^r 1771 We the subscribers have processioned every persons land in our precinct as followeth (vizt)
Between Wm Chaney and Francis Brizendine in the presence of Wm Chaney.
Between Francis Brizendine & Thomas Cox in the presence of Thomas Cox.
Between Francis Brizendine & Thomas Bush in the presence of Thomas Bush.
Between Thos Bush and John Vass in the presence of Thos. Bush.
Between Thos. Bush & Robt. James in the presence of Robt. James.
Between Robt. James & John Vass in the presence of Robt. James.
Between Robt. James & Philip Cheyney in the presence of Robt. James.
Between Philip Cheney & John Vass in the presence of John Vass.
Between Robt Man & Caty Johnson in the presence of John Man.
Between Robt. Man & Nathan Breadlove in the presence of John Mann.
Between Peter Trible & Caty Johnson in the presence of Peter Trible.
Between Peter Trible & Hugh Marshel in the presence of Peter Trible.
Between Robt. Mann & Allamon Breedlove in the presence of Peter Trible.
Between Peter Trible & Robt. Mann in the presence of Peter Trible.
Between Peter Trible & John Mann in the presence of Peter Trible.
Between Nathan Breedlove and John Mann in the presence of Peter Trible.
Between Philip Kid & Con^t Edmondson in the presence of John Mann.

Between Con Edmondson & John Rodden in the presence of John Mann.
Between Con.^t Edmondson & William Flitcher in the presence of John Mann.
Between Isaac Kid & William Flitcher in the presence of John Mann.
Between Robt Broocke and William Williams in the presence of John Mann.
Between Robt Broocke and Con Edmondson in the presence of John Mann.
Between Isaac Kid & Robt Broocke in the presence of John Mann.

[97]   [1771 Processioning]
Between Ezek.^l Byrom and Oze Byrom in the presence of John Byrom.
Between Oze Byrom and John Byrom in the presence of John Byrom.
Between John Byrom and William Flitcher in the presence of John Byrom.
Between William Fletcher and John Williams in the presence of William Fletcher.
Between John Williams & Thomas Gordon in the presence of John Williams.
Between Evan Davis and Isaac Sheridan in the presence of Evan Davis.
Between Evan Davis and Philip Kid in the presence of Philip Davis.
Between Evan Davis & James Webb in the presence of Philip Davis.
Between James Webb & John Hodges in the presence of John Hodges.
Between Richard Brizendine & John Hodges in the presence of John Hodges.
Between Richard Brizendine and Thomas Cox in the presence of Thomas Cox.
Between Thomas Cox & Philip Kid in the presence of Thomas Cox.
Between Thos. Cox & John Mann in the presence of Thos. Cox.

         Francis Brizendine
         John Brizendine
         John Dobbyns

8th   In obedience to an order made at Vestry held at Cap. 'James Edmondsons Piscataway Ferry on the 8th day of Octob.^r 1771. We the subscribers have processioned every persons land in our precinct except the line between John Maibell and William Ramseys orphan.

Begining the line between John Gude & Elizabeth Wright in presents of Ambrose Bohannon.

Between Elizabeth Wright & Saml Grissom also Grissom & William Ramseys orphan, between Samuel Grissom & John Taylors orphan, all in presents of John Davis & Josiah Minter.

The line between John Maibell & John Taylors orphans in presents of Josiah Minter.

Between Josiah Minter & Wm. Ramsey's orphan, between W^m. Fletcher & W^m. Ramseys orphan, between Josiah Minter and W^m. Fletcher, between W^m. Dunn and W^m. Fletcher, between William Dunn and Thomas Turner, between Wm Fletcher & Thomas Turner all in presents of Josiah Minter & Wm Dunn.

Between Thomas Dunn and Thomas Turner, between Thos Dunn & Wm Hays, between Wm Hays & Thos Dunn all in presents of John Turner & Thomas Turner. Between Isaac Jordan and Wm Hays, between Isaac Jordan and Evan Davis, between Isaac Jordan & Rachel Clark, between Isaac Jordan & Richard Williamson, between Isaac Jordan & Thomas Gordon, between Richard Williamson & Thos Turner, between Richd Williamson & Thos Gordon all processioned in presents of Elkanah Turner and Richard Williamson.

[98]   [1771 Processioning]
Between Thomas Gordon & Thomas Turner also Isaac Williamson & Thomas Turner, between Isaac Williamson and John Rodden processioned in presents of Isaac Williamson and James Gordon.

Also between John Rodden & William Davis between W^m. Davis and John Gude between John Rodden & John Gude, between John Rodden & Else Williamson between Else Williamson and John Gude in presents of Isaac Williamson & John Rodden and William Davis. Also between Thos. Gordon and Else Williamson in presents of James Gordon. Between W^m. Fletcher & John Gude in presents of W^m. Fletcher & Isaac Williamson. Also between Isaac Williamson & Else Williamson in presents of James Gordon & Isaac Williamson. Between Evan Davis and John Williamson between Evan Davis and Mary Watts, between John Williamson & Mary Webb, between John Williamson & William Prossor, all in presents of Evan Davis & John Williamson.

The line between Elizabeth Cooper and Thomas Williamson in presents of Thomas Williamson & Thomas Cox.
The line between John Brisley and Thomas Cox in presents of Thomas Cox and John Brizendine, all peaceably processioned by the subscribers.
   Octob[r] 1st. 1772   Phillip Kidd
            Thomas Gordon
            Isaac Jordan

9th A list of the Processioners

The line between Richard Brown and Francis Brown dec[d] in presents of William Dunn and Thomas Dennet, also the line between Thomas Dennet & Fran[s]. Brown in presents of Richard Brown & William Dunn, also the line between Thomas Dunn and Fran[s] Brown in presents of Richard and W[m] Dunn, also the line between W[m] Dunn & Fran[s]. Brown in presents of Richard Brown and Thomas Dennet. Also the line between W[m]. Dunn & Richard Brown in presents of Thomas Dennet & Richard Brown, also the line between Elizabeth Dunn and Thomas Henry Brooks in presents of James Gordon and Richard Brown, also the line between John Brooks and Williamson in presents of Thomas Henry Brooks & Richard Brown, also the line between Thomas Allen and John Brooke in presents of Thomas H[y]. Broocks and Richard Brown, also the line between John Broocks and Richard Brown, also the line between John Broocks and Mary Marlow in presents of Thos H[y]. Broocks and Reuben Marlow, also the line between Mary Marlow & Elizabeth Dunn in presents of Reuben Marlow & Richard Brown, also the line between Mary Marlow and Thomas Allen in presents of Wm Dunn and Wm. Marlow, also the line between Benjamin Dunn and Susanna Crow in presents of Isom Crow & Benjamin Dunn, also the line between Susanna Crow and Thomas Allen in presents of Benjamin Dunn & Isom Crow. Also the line between Susanna Crow and John Crow in presents of Isom Crow and John Brooks, also the line between Thomas Allen and John Crow in present of Benjamin Dunn & John Brooks, also the line between Richd Jeffries and Thomas Allen in presents of Benjamin Dunn and John Brooks, also the line between Thomas Allen & Tho[s] Miller in present of Benj[a] Dunn & John Brooks.

[99] [1771 Processioning]
Also the line between Williamson Williams & Thomas Allen in presents of Benjamin Dunn and John Brooks. The line between Luke Covington & Thomas Webb in presents of John Webb and Luke Covington, also the line between John Dickerson and Luke Covington in presents of Luke Covington & John Dickerson, also the line between William Webb and John Dickerson in presents of John Webb and John Dickerson, also the line between John Webb & William Webb in presents of John Webb and John Dickerson, also the line between Esther Dobbins & John Webb in presents of John Dobbins and John Webb, also the line between John Webb and John Williamson in presents of John Webb and John Williamson, also the line between John Williamson and W^m. Webb in presents of John Webb and John Williamson, also the line between Thomas Webb and John Williamson, also the line between Thomas Webb and John Dickerson in present of John Webb and John Dickerson. Also the line between Mary Marlow and Thomas Webb in presents of John Webb and John Dickerson, also the line between Thomas Webb & Elizabeth Dunn in presents of John Dickerson and John Webb, also the line between Thomas Webb and Richard Brown in presents of John Dickerson and John Webb, also the line between W^m. Webb and Richard Brown in presents of John Webb and Richard Brown.

William Dunn
Richard Brown
Thomas Dennett

[100] [1771 Processioning]
Pursuant to an order of Vestry of the Parish of South Farnham Wee the subscribers have processioned the lands in our precincts as followeth dec^r 2
1 Line between James Banks and Josiah Minter in presents of Thomas Wood, Josiah Minter and Wm Dunn Junr B.
1 Line between James Banks and John Gorden in presents of Thos Wood Josiah Minter and Wm Dunn Junr B.
1 Line between John Boughan and Thomas Wood in presents of Josiah Minter John Chatten and Wm Dunn Junr B.

[Dec] 9th.
2 lines between James Banks and W^m. Dunn B. in presents John Minter

and Tho⁵. Allen.
1 Line between Wᵐ Dunn B. and Nathˡ. Dunn in presents of Josiah Minter and Tho⁵. Allen.
2 Lines between John Edmondson and Benjᵃ. Jones in presents of Josiah Minter and Tho⁵. Allen.
2 Lines between Tho⁵. Allen and Benjᵃ. Jones in presents of Josiah Minter, James Edmondson and James Booker.
1 Line between Benjᵃ. Jones and James Booker in presents of Josiah Minter and Tho⁵. Allen.

10ᵗʰ.
1 Line between Henry Purkins and Jacob Sherwood in presents of Capᵗ. Tho⁵. Roane, Capᵗ. Wᵐ. Roane and Tho⁵. Wood.
1 Line between Capᵗ. Tho⁵. Roane and Jacob Sherwood in presents of Capᵗ. Wᵐ. Roane Henry Purkins & Wᵐ. Perkins.
2 Lines between Capᵗ. Tho⁵. Roane and Danˡ. Hodgett in presents of Capᵗ. Wᵐ. Roane Tho⁵. Wood Henry Purkins and Wᵐ Purkins.
1 Corner Red at the head of a gulley between Capᵗ. Tho⁵. Roane and Hugh Wilson in presents of Capᵗ. Wᵐ. Roane Tho⁵. Wood Henry Purkins and Wᵐ. Purkins.
1 Line between Capᵗ. Tho⁵. Roane and John Croxton in presents of Tho⁵. Wood.
1 Line between Capᵗ. Tho⁵. Roane and Tho⁵. Croxton in presents of Capᵗ. Wᵐ. Roane Tho⁵. Wood Henry Purkins and Wᵐ. Purkins.
1 Line between Tho⁵. Croxton and James Booker in presents of Cap.ᵗ Tho⁵. Roane Capᵗ. Wᵐ. Roane Thomas Wood Henry Purkins & Wᵐ. Purkins.

The other lands in our precinct not processioned the freeholders not giving their attendance.
        James Booker
        William Dunn B.
        James Bankes

12ᵗʰ
The land in the precincts not processioned by reason of Joseph Ryland & Samuel Allen being not able to attend.
        Richard Holt Junʳ

[101] [this page is deliberately blank]
[probably reserved for the returns of precincts 13 and 14]

[102]   [1771 Processioning]
15th Pursuant to an order of the Vestry of South Farnham Parish appointing the subscribers processioners we have accordingly processioned the following lines.

Decr 18 & 21 1771

Begining between John Meador & Alex^r Smith & then between John Meador and Richd Meador down to Warings Old Mill Swamp and then between Thomas, John & Richd Meador and then between Richd Meador and James Gatewood and then between James Gatewood & Thos Allen and then between John Burnett and Thomas Wood down to Boughans Mill Swamp in presence of all parties. Given under our hands.

        Rich^d. Thos. Haile
        Henry Kidd
        Thos. Allan

[no return for 16th precinct]

[103]   [1771 Processioning]
17th In obedience to the within order we the subscribers have not processioned any of the land in our precinct all being joyning to orphans land therefore not processioned.

        Wm Edmondson
        Alex^r Smith

18th Pursuant to an order of the worshipful Vestry of South Farnham Parish appointing the subscribers processioners in their precinct agreable to which order we processioned the line between Mr Benjamin [Waggener] & Nathan Waggener, also the line between Mr Benjamin Wagginer & Robt Sd Waring, also the line between Robt Sd Waring & Nathan Waggener, also the line between R. P. Waring and Richard Meadors which is by the parties acknowledgment the meanders of Hoskins Creek, also the line between Mr Alex^r Smith & Nathan Waggener, present Mr Benjamin Waggener at the processioning all the above lines.

We also processioned the line between Mr McDuff and R. P. Waring present Mr John Smith, all other lines in our precinct are bounds of orphans lands so that we did not procession them except the line between Capt Wm Roane & Mr McDuff which by consent of Capt Wm Roane and Doctr Mortimer attorney for sd McDuff was putt off for a survey which they have not yet had. As witness our hands this 29th. of Decr. 1771.
R. P. Waring
Nathan Waggener

19th Pursuant to an order of the Vestry of South Farnham Parish We the subscribers have processioned the lines mentioned Between John Upshaw & Thomas Sthreshly present John Upshaw, also between Thomas Sthreshly and John Hill the s^d Hill present, also betwen the s^d Hill & Sarah Rennolds present John Rennolds, John Rennolds Junr and Sthreshly Rennolds.

Also between the s^d. Rennolds and Sthreshly.
Also between the s^d. Rennolds and Elizabeth Rennolds.
Also between the s^d. Eliz^a. Rennolds & Thomas Sthreshly.
Also between the s^d. Eliz^a. Rennolds and John Upshaw Gent.
Also between the s^d. Eliz^a. Rennolds and Mary Gatewood present Augustine & Richard Gatewood.
Also a line between the sd John Upshaw & Mary Gatewood.
Also a line between the sd Mary Gatewood & Wm Gatewood.
Also a line between the sd John Upshaw & Wm Gatewood absent Augustine & Richard Gatewood.
Also a line between Wm Webb & the above sd Sthreshly nobody present but the parties.
Thomas Sthreshly
William Webb
Erasmus Jones

Truly entered Henry Vass Clk of the Vestry

****

[104] [1771 Processioning]
At a Vestry held for South Farnham Parish at Capt James Edmondsons Piscataway Ferry on the 13th day of Octob^r 1773
    Present
    The Revd Mr Cruden
    William Roane } Church Wardens
    James Campbell

John Upshaw, Thomas Roane, William Montague, William Young, Archibald Ritchie, Meriwether Smith and James Webb, Gent.

The Processioners Returns Exam^d in Vestry.
                Alex^r Cruden
                James Webb } Ch Ward^{ns}
                James Campbell

Truly Registered p Henry Vass Clk of ye Vestry

****

[105] [1775 Processioning]
At a Vestry held for the Parrish of South Farnham at Tappahannock on the 27th day of Octob^r 1775.

Present
William Smith Church Warden, John Upshaw, Thomas Roane, Arch^d Ritchie, William Roane, James Edmondson & William Young Gent.

Pursuant to an order of Court for the County of Essex bearing date October Court Anno Dommy one thousand seven hundred seventh & five Where by it is ordered that the Vestry of each parish within the said county divide their parishes into so many precincts as the them shall seem most convenient for processioning every particular persons land in the several parishes and appoint the particular times for processioning, likewise appoint two intelligent honest freeholders at least of every precinct to see such processioning performed, and take and return to the Vestry an account of every persons lands they shall procession and of the persons present at the same and what land in their precincts they shall fail to procession and of the particular reasons of such failure.

This present Vestry do their fore divide the parish of South Farnham into nineteen precincts, and it is ordered that Robert Clark Richard Street and Henry Street or any two procession every persons land in their precinct begining at the lower end of Essex County and runing to the Gleab Creek from thence to M^r. Leonard Hills Quarter on the Dragon begining the tenth day of November and to finish by the tenth day of Decemb^r. and to make their return as the law directs.

2nd Ordered that Ab^r. Saunders and Charles Saunders and William Mullin or any two procession every persons land in their precinct begining at M^r. Leonard Hills Quarter on the Dragon from thence to Joshua Boughtons and so to the Dragon and from thence to M^{rs}. Adams Quarter on the River Side begining the fifteenth day of Novem^r and to finish by the last day of the same month and to make their return as the law directs.

3rd Ordered that Thomas Newbill, Andrew Allen and John Broocke or any two procession every persons land in their precinct begining at Joshua Boughtons from thence to Capt. James Webbs Quarter on the Old Mill Swamp that leads to Piscataway Creek from thence to William Chaneys on the Dragon begining the twentyith day of November and to finish by the twenty sixth day of December and to make their return as the Law directs.

4th Ordered that Richard Philips Reuben Broocke & William Shephard or any two do procession every person land in their precinct from Mrs Adams's to Gatewoods Creek by Henry Youngs so along the Road to Joshua Boughtons begining the twenty second day of November and to finish by the twenty second day of December and to make their return as the law directs.

[106]   [1775 Processioning]
5th Ordered that Richard Jeffries Thomas Evans and Thomas Johnson

or any two procession every persons land in their precinct from Mr Gatewoods land near Mrs Mary Youngs from thence to Capt James Webbs Quarter by his Mill from thence along the Swamp to Piscataway Creek and down the Creek to the Ferry thence down the Road to the beginning beginning the twenty sixth day of November and to finish by the twenty sixth day of December and to make their return as the law directs.

6th Ordered that William Gatewood Junr William Young Junr & Thomas Cauthorn or any two procession every persons land in their precinct from William Gatewoods land near Mrs. Mary Youngs from thence to Creek where John Philips formerly lived so down the Creek, thence including all the lands between the Main Road and the River to Piscataway Creek beginning the twenty eight day of November and to finish by the first day of January and to make their return as the law directs.

7th Ordered that Francis Brizendine John Brizendine and John Webb J^r or any two procession every persons land in their precinct begining at William Chaneys on the Dragon from thence to the head of Covingtons Mill Swamp and down the Swamp to Mrs. E[l]izabeth Wrights Landing from thence up the Road by Thomas Williamson to William Cheaneys begining the third day of December and to finish by the twelfth day of January and to make their return as the law directs.

8th Ordered that Philip Kidd Thomas Gorden & Evan Davis or any two procession every persons land in their precinct begining at M^rs. Elizabeth Wrights Land and so up Piscataway Creek to the Old Mill from [thence] along the Road to M^r. James Webb Ordinary from thence down the branch to the Dragon and to William Cheneys from thence to Mrs. Eliz^a. Wrights Landing begining the fifth day of December and to finish by the fifteenth day of January and to make their return as the law directs.

9th Ordered that William Dunn (white), Thomas Dennett and Richard Brown or any two procession every persons land in their precinct begining at Mathews Bridge from thence to the Road and down the Road to Elliots old field from thence to the head of the Dragon & down the Dragon to a branch below John Webb Junr. from thence up the branch to M^r. Webbs Ordinary and along the Road to Mathew's Bridge begining the tenth day of December and to finish by the last day of January and to make their return as the law directs.

10th   Ordered that William Howerton, Heritage Howerton & Richard St. John or any two procession every persons land in their precinct beginning between the two branches of the Dragon from thence up the Main Road that divideth Essex County from King & Queen County begining the twelfth day of December and to finish by the last day of January and to make their return as the law directs.

11th   Ordered that William Dunn (B) James Booker & Thomas Wood or any two procession every persons land in their precinct begining at Hails Bridge from thence down the Road to the Long Reach Road from thence to the head of Fishers Mill Swamp and down the Swamp to Mathews Bridge from thence along the Road to the Old Mill from thence up the Swamp to Hales Bridge begining the tenth day of November and to finish by the tenth day of December and to make their return as the law directs.

12th   Ordered that Thomas Ryland Richard Holt Ju^r and Joseph Bohannon or any two procession every persons land in their precinct begining at Hails Bridge from thence to the Long Reach Road from thence up the Road to the dividing line of the County from thence to the head of Piscataway Swamp and down the Swamp to Hails Bridge begining the fifteenth day of November and to finish by the fifteenth day of December and to make their return as the law directs.

[107]   [1775 Processioning]
13th   Ordered that John Edmondson J^r John Games & John Burk or any two procession every persons land in their precinct begining at Hoskins Bridge from thence to Piscatawy Ferry and so down each creek to the River begining the twentieth day of November and to finish by the twentieth day of December and to make their return as the law directs.

14th   Ordered that John Kircherval, John Boughan Junr & Richard Burck or any two procession every persons land in their precinct begining at Hoskins Bridge and so down to Piscataway Ferry from thence up to Boughans Mill and up to Whites Run Bridge begining the twenty second day of November and to finish by the twenty second day of December and to make their return as the law directs.

15th Ordered that Richard Thomas Haile, Henry Kidd & Thomas Allen or any two procession every persons land in their precinct between Boughans Mill across to Warrings Mill and to Hails Bridge and across to Warrings Mill Swamp begining the twenty sixth day of December and to make their return as the law directs.

16th Ordered that Thomas Dix, William Latane and Andrew Gatewood or any two procession every persons land in their precinct between Hails Bridge and Warrings Old Mill Swamp and up to the dividing line of Essex County from King & Queen County begining the twenty sixth day of November and to finish by the first day of January and to make their return as the law directs.

17th Ordered that Augustine Moore, Whitehead Coleman and Benjamin Waggoner or any two procession every persons land in their precinct which is to say the land in the Mill Neck from Capt. Smiths across to Fauntleroys late dwelling plantation begining the third day of December and to finish by the twelfth day of January and to make their return as the law directs.

18th Orderd that Robt. P. Warring John Rennolds and Nathan Waggoner or any two procession every persons land in their precinct from Smiths and Fauntleroys to Warrings Old Mill from thence across to Capt. William Roanes land formerly Tandys begining the fifth day of December and to finish by the fifteenth day of January and to make their return as the law directs.

19th Ordered that Thomas Sthreshley, William Webb and Erasmus Jones or any two procession every persons land in their precinct from Warrings Old Mill and Roans land formerly Tandys to the uper end of the parrish begining the tenth day of December and to finish by the last day of January and to make their return as the law directs.

William Smith Ch Warden

[108] [this page is deliberately blank]

[109] [1779 Processioning]
At a vestry held for South Farnham Parrish at Capt James Edmondsons Piscataway Ferry the first day of October 1779.

Present Newman Brokenbrow
        Church Warden

M^r. John Upshaw, Samuel Peachey, William Roane, William Young, John Beale & John Edmondson ye Gen^t.

Pursuant to an order court for the County of Essex bareing date August 1779 whereby it is orderd that eh Vestry of each parrish in the said County divide the precincts as to themselves shall seem most convenient for processioning every particular persons land in the several parrishes and appoint the seeral particular times for processioning likewise appoint two intelligent freeholders at least of every precinct to see such processioning perform'd and take and return to the vestry an account of every persons land they shall procession and of the persons present at the same and what land in their repcincts they shall faile to procession and of the particular reasons of such failure.

This present Vestry do divide the parrish of South Farnham into nineteen precincts and it is order'd that Richd Street, John Yarrington & John Oweing or any two procession every persons land in their precinct begining at the lower end of Essex County and ru[n]ing to the Gleab Creek from thence to Mr. Hills Quarter on the Dragon begining the tenth day of November and to finish by the tenth day of December and to make their return as the law directs.

2^d Order^d that James Dejarnett Thos. Boughton & Charles Sanders do procession the land in their precinct begining at Mr. Leonard Hills Quarter on the Dragon from thence to the land of Joshua Boughton Decd & so to the Dragon from thence to M^{rs}. Adams Quarter on the River Side begining the fifteenth day of November & to finish by the last day of the same month and to make their return as the law directs.

3ᵈ Orderᵈ that John Brooke Henry Newbill & Nathanell Newbill or any two of them do procession every persons land in their precinct begining at William Youngs from thence to Capt. James Webb Quarter on the Old Mill Swamp that leads to Piscataway Creek from thence to William Chaneys on the Dragon begiing the twentieth day of November & finishing the twelveᵗʰ day of December and to make their return as the law dreicts.

4ᵗʰ Orderᵈ that Richᵈ Phillips, Reuben Broocke, & William Shephard or any two do procession every persons land in their precinct from Mʳˢ. Adams to Gatewoods Creek by Henry Youngs thence up the back to the Main Road by Mrs. Mary Youngs so [a]long the Road to Joshua Boughtons decd begining the twenty second day of November & to finish by the twenty second of December and to make their return as the law directs.

5ᵗʰ Orderᵈ that Thoˢ. Johnson John Patterson & Richᵈ Jeffries do procession every persons land in their precinct begining at Henry Gardners and from thence to Capt. James Webbs Quarter by his Mill & so [a]long the Swamp to Piscataway Creek and down the Creek to the Ferry thence down the Road to the begining the twenty sixth day of November & to finish by the twenty sixth day of December & to make their return as the law directs.

[110]   [1779 Processioning]
6ᵗʰ Orderᵈ. that William Gatewood William Young jr & Thomas Evans or any two of them do procession every persons land in their precinct from William Gatewoods land near Mʳˢ. Mary Young from thence to the Creek where John Phillips formerly livᵈ so down the creek including all the land between the Main Road & the River to Piscataway Creek begining the twenty eight day of November & finish ing the first day of January and to make their return as the law directs.

7ᵗʰ Orderᵈ. that William Howerton Isaac Jordon & Thoˢ. Williamson or any two do procession every persons land in their precent begining at William Shaneys [Chaney] land on the Dragon from thence to the head of Covingtons Mill Swamp & to Mrs. Wrights Landing as was from thence up the Road by Thomas Williamsons to William Chaneys from thence to the s^d. Wrights Landing formerly begining the fifth day of December & finishing the fifteenth day of January and to make their return as the law directs.

8th Order^d. that Phillip Kidd Evan Davis & Richd Broocke or any two do procession every persons land in their precinct begining at M^{rs}. Wrights Landing formerly and so up Piscataway Creek to the Old Mill then along the Road to M^r. William Havertons ordinary from thence down the branch to the Dragon & to William Chaneys & from thence to Mrs. Wrights Landing begining the fifth day of December & to finish the fifteenth day of Jany. and to make their return as the law directs.

9th Order^d. that William Dunn W: Rich^d. Brown & John Broocke son of Thom^s Henry Brooke or any two do procession every persons land in their precinct begining at Matthews Bridge & from thence to the Road to Elliots old field from thence to the head of the Dragon and down the Dragon to a branch below John Webb & from thence up the branch to Mr. William Havertons & along the Road to Matthews Bridge begining the tenth day of December & finishing by the last day of January and to make their return as the law directs.

10th Order^d. that Heritage Haverton Rich^d St. John & William Covington or any two do procession every persons land in their precinct being between the two branches of the Dragon from thence up the Main Road that divides Essex County from King & Queen begining the twelfth day of December and to finish by the last day of January and to make their return as the law directs.

11th Order^d. that Thos. Wood William Edmondson & Jo^s. Croxton or any two do procession every persons land in their precincts begining at Hails Bridge from thence down the road to the Long Reach Road from thence to the head of Fishers Mill Swamp & down the Swamp to Matthews Bridge from thence along the Road to the Old Mill from thence up the Swamp to Hails Bridge begining the tenth day of November & to finish by the tenth day of December & to make their return as the law directs.

12th Order^d. that Joseph Bohannon, John Coleman & Benj^a Jones or any two do procession all the lands in their precincts begining at Hailes Bridge from thence to the Long Reach Road from thence up the Road to the dividing line of the County from thence to the head of Piscataway Swamp to Hails Bridge begining the fifteenth day of November & to finish by the fifteenth day of December and to make their return as the law directs.

[111]   [1779 Processioning]
13th Order^d. that William Gatewood Richard Burk & John Burk or any two of them do procession every persons land in their precincts begining at Hoskins Bridge from thence to Piscataway Ferry & so down each creek to the River begining the twentieth day of November & to finish by the twentieth day of December and to make their return as the law directs.

14th Order^d. that John Boughan John Kershevel and Thos. Smith or any two of them do procession every persons land in their preceints begining at Hoskins Bridge and so down to Piscataway Ferry from thence up to Boughtons Mill & so up to Whites Run Bridge begining the twenty second day of November and to finish by the second day of December and to make their return as the law directs.

15th Order^d. that Rich^d. T Haile Henry Kidd & Thos. Allen or any two of them do procession every persons land in their precincts begining between Boughans Mill & across to Warings Mill Swamp begining the twenty sixth day of December and to make their return as the law directs.

16th Order^d. that William Latane Joseph Gatewood & Reuben Garnett or any two do procession every persons land in their precincts begining between Hails Bridge & Warings Old Mill Swamp and up the dividing line of Essex County from King & Queen County begining the twenty sixth day of November & to finish by the twenty sixth day of December and to make their return as the law directs.

17th Order^d. that Gideon Ship Benj^a Waggener & Richd Allen or any two of them do procession every persons land in their precinct that is to say the land that is in the Mill Neck from Alex^r. Smith decd to Fauntleroys late dwelling plantation begining the third day of December & to finish by the twentieth day of January and to make their return as the law directs.

18th Order^d. that John Reynolds Haraway Owing & Henry Hipkins or any two do procession every persons land in their precincts from Smiths and Fauntleroys & Warings Old Mill from thence across to Coll. Roanes land formerly Tandys begining the fifth day of December & to finish by the fifteenth day of January and to make their return as the law directs.

19th Order^d. that Thomas Sthreshly Erasmus Jones and William Webb or any two procession every persons land in their precinct from Wareings Old Mill & Coll. Roanes land formerly Tandies to the upper end of the parrish begining the tenth day December & to finish by the last day of January and to make their return as the law directs.

Newman Brokenbrow
Church Warden

Truly registered per J Purkins Clk the Vestry

****

Appendices

APPENDIX A

PARISH OFFICIALS

COLONIAL MINISTERS

1684-1686	Samuel Dudley
1686-1690	Duell Pead
1701-1733	Lewis Latane
1735-1736	Henry Shorthose
1739-1744	William Phillips
1747	William Stuart
1751-1776	Alexander Cruden
1776-1779	no minister

VESTRYMEN

Vestrymen served as a committee, directing the running of the church business. Only the years of service during processioning years are known.

John Beale	1779
N. Brockenbrough	1779
James Campbell	1771
Isaac Clements	1759
John Clements	1755,56,60,64
William Covington	1739,43,55,56,59,60
William Daingerfield	1743,44,52,59
James Edmondson	1775
John Edmondson	1779
James Mills	1756
Abraham Montague	1740
William Montague	1759,64,73
Alexander Parker	1740,43

Samuel Peachey	1771,79
James Rennolds	1739,40
John Richards	1771
Archibald Ritchie	1764,71,73,75
Thomas Roane	1764,71,73,75
William Roane	1739,40,44,52,55,56,75,79
John Robinson	1739
Isaac Scandrett	1739,43,55,56
Francis Smith	1755,56,60
Meriwether Smith	1771,73
Nicholas Smith	1739,40,43,44,55,56
John Upshaw	1752,55,56,59,60,71,73,75,79
John Vass	1739,40,43,44
Thomas Waring	1752,55,56
James Webb	1743,44,52,55,56,59,60,64,71,73
Henry Young	1743,44
William Young	1759,60,64,71,73,75,79

CHURCH WARDENS

The church wardens acted as executives for the church. Usually two church wardens served at a time. Only the years of service during processioning years are known.

1739	John Robinson
1740	William Covington, William Daingerfield
1743	William Roane, Francis Smith
1744	William Roane, Francis Smith
1747	Alexander Parker, William Stuart, John Vass
1751	John Clements, John Vass
1752	John Clements, John Vass
1755	William Daingerfield, James Webb
1756	William Daingerfield, James Webb
1759	Francis Smith

1760   John Clements, William Montague
1763   John Upshaw, William Young
1764   John Upshaw, Samuel Peachey
1771   William Montague, William Roane
1773   James Campbell, William Roane, James Webb
1775   William Smith

CLERKS OF THE VESTRY

These are the men whose handwriting is found in this volume. Fortunately, both John Vass and Henry Vass had very legible handwriting and fairly consistent spelling.

John Vass	1739,40,43,47,51,52
Henry Vass	1755,56,63,71,73
J. Purkins	1779

APPENDIX B

GLOSSARY and ABBREVIATIONS

Clk	clerk
Col^o, Co^{ll}	colonel
dec'd	deceased
Ex^a	examined
possession	procession; various spellings
pr	per, by
vizt	vidilicet, meaning 'that is to say,' or 'namely'

BIBLIOGRAPHY

Arritt, Anne B. "A List of Freeholders that Voted in the Election of Burgesses for the County of Essex on the Ninth Day of July 1765," *The Virginia Genealogist.* Vol 6 (1968), p 67-72.

Blomquist, Ann. *The Vestry Book of Southam Parish, Cumberland County, VA 1745-1792.* Westminster, MD: Willow Bend Books, 2002.

Chamberlayne, C. G. *The Vestry Book of St. Paul's Parish, Hanover County, VA 1706-1786.* Richmond, VA: The Library Board, 1940.

Cocke, Charles Francis. *Parish Lines, Diocese of VA.* Richmond, VA: VA State Library, 1967.

Dorman, John Frederick. *Essex County VA Wills, Bonds, Inventories, Etc. 1722-1730.* Washington DC, 1961.

Gaidmore, Gerald. *A Guide to the Church Records in the Library of Virginia.* Richmond, VA: The Library of Virginia, 2001.

Hall, Wilmer. *The Vestry Book of the Upper Parish, Nansemond County, VA 1743-1793.* Richmond, VA: VA State Library, 1949.

Hening, William W. *The Statutes at Large, Being a Collection of All the Laws of Virginia.* Richmond, VA.

Hopewell, John S. "Essex County Voters in 1769," *The Virginia Genealogist.* Vol. 46, No. 3 (Jul/Sep 2002), p 167-170.

Hopewell, John S. "Presbyterians Certify Their Presence in Essex County, Virginia, 1758, " *The Virginia Genealogist.* Vol. 42, No. 2 (Apr/June 1998), p 146-147.

Hopewell, John S. "Two Tithable Lists from Essex County ca 1764-1765," *The Virginia Genealogist.* Vol. 46, No. 3 (Jul/Sep 2002), p 163-177.

Mason, George Carrington. "The Colonial Churches of Essex and Richmond Counties," *The Virginia Magazine of History and Biography.* Vol. 53 (1945), p 3-20.

Mead, William. *Old Churches, Ministers, and Families of Virginia.* Genealogical Publishing Company, 1966.

Nicklin, John B. C. "Essex County: An Annotated Copy of the Rent Roll of 1704," *William and Mary Quarterly,* Second Series. Vol 21. (1941), p 397-405.

Nicklin, John B. C. "Quit Rent Roll for the Year 1715, Essex County, Virginia," *William and Mary Quarterly,* Second Series. Vol. 18 (1938), p 203-206.

"A Poll Taken for the Electing Burgesses in Essex County in Tappahannock 1768," *The Virginia Genealogist.* Vol. 6 (1968), p 84-88.

Shepard, E. Lee. *A History of St. Paul's Episcopal Church.* Richmond, VA: Dietz, 2001.

Slaughter, James B. *Settlers, Southerners, Americans, A History of Essex County, VA 1608-1984.* Tappahannock, VA: Essex County Board of Supervisors, 1995.

Weis, Frederick L. *The Colonial Clergy of Virginia, North Carolina, and South Carolina.* Boston, MA, 1955.

INDEX

Variant spellings should be checked. Names may appear more than once on a page. Some surnames were spelled differently than they are now, for example, Broocke. Because only the microfilm was available for verification, it is very likely that there were mistakes made in reading names, especially ones with superscripts,. Examples of problems are M^r. and M^{rs}. Adams, Abr^m and Alex^r, Barker and Basket, Bush and Burk, Bourn and Brown, Taylor and Tayloe, etc.

Abbott, Jacob 11,38,59
Ackres, see Acres
Acres, Jane 36
Acres, Robert 10,16,36,79,103, 104,121
Adams 131
Adams, Charles 82
Adams, Mr. 100,118
Adams, Mrs. 2,11,28,38,50,54, 54,62,70,93,100,101,110, 118,126,145,149,150
Adams, Orphans 47
Adams, Richard 76,117,131, 133
Adams, Tabitha 59
Akers, see Acres
Akres, James 66
Allen, Andrew 100,111,126, 132,133,145
Allen, Benjamin 13,45,57,67, 73,90,96,110,114,124
Allen, Benjamin Jr 43
Allen, Charles 5
Allen, Elizabeth 83,105,123
Allen, James 34,57,66,73,88,96, 109

Allen, John 4,16,17,21,34,42, 43,81,85,88
Allen, John Jr 53
Allen, Orphans 81,86
Allen, Richard 152
Allen, Samuel 24,41,52,56,65, 72,84,85,95,108,112,127,141
Allen, Thomas 128,139,140, 141,142,148,152
Allen, Widow 86
Allen, William 20,85
Allen, Zacharias 20
Allen, Zachary 34
Amiss, Joseph 45
Amiss, William 98,116
Anderson, Joseph 14
Armistead, Capt. 9
Armistead, Henry 130
Armistead, John 59,64,76,99
Armstead, see Armistead
Armstrong, Elizabeth 25
Armstrong, John 5,13,25,31,43, 45,53,57,73,96,113,114,124
Atkins, James 11,106,107
Attkins, see Atkins
Attwood, Francis 30,39,42

Attwood, John 20
Aylett 65,66
Aylett, William 23,24,40,41
Aylott, see Aylett

Back Road 2,28,50,54,70,93, 111
Baker, Amy 12,25
Baker, Henry 64
Baker, Jane 81,123
Baker, Jean 105
Baker, John 39
Ball, Abner 84,85
Ball, Edmond 85
Ball, Henry 85
Ball, James 84
Ball, John 23,24,25,41,65,84,85
Ball, Mark 85
Banks, James 56,68,72,83,95, 107,108,112,127,140,141
Barcley, Patt 44
Barker, Thomas 23,56,66
Barnes, Thomas 89
Baskett, William 6,33
Bates, John 13
Baylor, John 16
Beal 118
Beal, Capt. 38
Beale, John 116,117,131,149, 156
Beale, Mr. 100
Beale, Richard 2
Beale, Thomas 100
Beale, William 8,11,58,59,76
Beaver Dam 26
Belfield, Thomas 22,35
Bell, Thomas 16,17,20,34,42
Bennet, William 84

Bennett, John 30,34,35
Bennett, Joseph 30
Beverley, Christopher 13,45
Beverley, William 90
Billips, John 22,35
Bird 101
Bird, Capt. 47
Bird, George 102,118,133
Bird, Hannah 59
Bird, John 11
Bird, Mr. 12
Bird, Orphans 101,117
Bird, Philemon 76
Birom, see Byrom
Blackley, George 130
Bland, Theodore 17
Blatt, John 101,132
Blatt, Thomas 37
Blaxton, Acquile 13
Bohannan, Ambrose 138
Bohannan, Elizabeth 39,40
Bohannan, Joseph 147,152
Bohannan, William 9
Bohannon, see Bohannan
Bomar, Alexander 33,132
Bomar, Edward 12,32,61,77, 100,101
Bomar, Peter 32
Bomar, William 101,132
Bomer, see Bomar
Bond, William 111,126,132, 133
Boog, Mr. 36
Booker, James 65,83,108,112, 124,127,141,147
Boughan 142
Boughan, Abner 18

Boughan, Francis 24,25,108, 124
Boughan, Henry 18,65
Boughan, James 3,15,16,18,23, 29,30,42,64,71,80,95,107, 108
Boughan, James Jr 37,51,55
Boughan, John 13,18,35,59, 66,83,95,108,124,140,152
Boughan, John Jr 147
Boughan, Sarah 18
Boughans Ferry 30
Boughans Mill 4,20,30,52,56, 57,72,73,95,96,113,128,147, 148,152
Boughans Mill Swamp 142
Boughton 26
Boughton, Isaac 101
Boughton, John 1,11,12,28,39, 50,54,59,61,76,99,100,101, 117,131,133
Boughton, John Jr 76,117
Boughton, Joshua 1,2,11,12,28, 32,39,47,50,54,59,61,62,70, 76,77,93,99, 100,111,117, 118,125,126,131,133,145, 149,150
Boughton, Thomas 131,149
Boughton, William 59,101
Boughtons Mill 128,152
Bourne, John 25,43,46,53
Bouten, see Boughton
Bowlers Ferry 2,28
Bowlware, William 11
Bradberry, William 17,22
Brasher, Thomas 52
Braxton, George 23,24,41,65
Braxton, Mr. 85
Braxton, Orphans 65

Bray, see Brey
Brazindine, see Brizendine
Breadlove, see Breedlove
Breedlove, Allaman 120,136
Breedlove, Charles 10,37,39
Breedlove, Nathan 103,120, 121,136
Breedlove, William 37
Brett, John 80
Brey, Charles 95,108,109,113, 128
Brezendine, Bresendine, see Brizendine
Bridges, see each name Hailes, Hoskins, Mathews, Meadors, Whites Run
Bridgforth, Thomas 98
Brim, John 131
Brisendine, Brisondine, see Brizendine
Brisley, John 139
Britt, John 80
Brizendine, Francis 61,71,77, 79,94,103,111,121,126,132, 136,137,146
Brizendine, John 79,104,105, 111,121,124,126,137,139, 146
Brizendine, Mary 16,36
Brizendine, Richard 32,37,137
Brockenbrough, Newman 132,149,153,156
Brokenbrow, see Brockenbrough
Broock, Broocks, see Broocke
Broocke, Christopher 131,133
Broocke, Isaac 61,78,102

Broocke, John 8,32,47,48,61, 62,77,93,101,102,111,118, 119,126,132,139,140,145, 150,151
Broocke, Jonathan Radford 108
Broocke, Leonard 133
Broocke, Mary 119, 121
Broocke, Peter 34,39,61,77, 102,117,130
Broocke, Philip 101
Broocke, Richard 151
Broocke, Reuben 132,133,145, 150
Broocke, Robert 25,137
Broocke, Samuel 8,47,48,61,62, 77,101,102,118
Broocke, Thomas 2,11,12,28, 32,33,34,47,61,71,77,79,83, 94,100,103,108,132
Broocke, Thomas Henry 65, 123,139,151
Broocke, William 6,8,12,32,34, 47,50,54,60,61,62,70,73,77, 89,96,100,101,117,118,130, 132,133
Broocke, William Jr 77,125
Broocking, Robert 35,36
Brook, Brooke, Brooks, see Broocke
Brown, Francis 18,80,81,105, 139
Brown, Henry 18,83,108
Brown, Hezekiah 83
Brown, John 18
Brown, Keziah 83,108

Brown, Richard 9,29,40,51,55, 64,71,81,82,94,105,106,112, 123,124,127,139,140,146, 151
Brown, John 31
Bucker, see Booker
Buford, Thomas 33
Buford, William 6,33,74
Burck, Burke, see Burk
Burk, John 147,152
Burk, Richard 128,147,152
Burk, Thomas 13,56,66,95,109
Burnet, Benjamin 87
Burnet, Charles 8
Burnet, James 87
Burnet, John 12,20,66,88,128, 142
Burnet, John Jr 87,113
Burnet, John Sr 87
Burnet, Joseph 20,52,66,72,95, 109,113
Burnet, Thomas 4,21,34,87
Burnet, William 87
Burnett, see Burnet
Bush 26,103
Bush, B 37
Bush, Bibby 8,10,29,37,51
Bush, Elizabeth 129
Bush, John 1,6,7,28,34,37,49, 60,75,98,115
Bush, John Jr 60,98
Bush, Richard 10,11,16,98
Bush, Reuben 129,130
Bush, Richard 2
Bush, Thomas 30,35,52,66,72, 120,121,136
Bushnell, Margaret 48
Byram, see Byrom

Byrom, Elizabeth 103
Byrom, Ezekiel 103,137
Byrom, James 37
Byrom, John 119,137
Byrom, Mary 67
Bryom, Orphans 119
Byrom, Oze 137

Callicoat, James 7,12
Callicoat, William 7
Calton, Ambrose 100
Cammell, John 14,38
Campbell, James 125,130,133, 144,156,158
Carflaphere[?], James 64
Carlton, Robert 117
Carlton, Thomas 116
Carroll, William 3,9
Cauthan, see Cauthorn
Cauthorn, Henry 32,78,111, 126,134,135
Cauthorn, James 63,78,102, 103,107
Cauthorn, John 62,78
Cauthorn, Richard 14,26,39
Cauthorn, Robert 109
Cauthorn, Thomas 2,14,28,29, 50,54,55,70,71,93,94,111, 126,134,135,136,146
Cauthorn, Vincent 39,55,78,63, 102,134,135
Cauthorn, William 78
Cauthorn, Williamson 79
Chamberlain, John 19,44,52, 56,66
Chaney, see Cheney
Charles, Chating (Chatten) 115,130,131
Chatten, John 140

Cheek, see Chick
Cheek, John 23
Cheney, John 2,12,33,61,77, 100,127
Cheney, Orphans 132
Cheney, Philip 132,136
Cheney, William 2,3,12,28,29, 32,37,50,51,54,55,63,70,71, 93,94,103,111,112,121,126, 127,136,145,146,150,151
Cheyney, Chenie, see Cheney
Chick, John 22
Church 87
Church Spring 87
Church Swamp 87
Clark, Charles 23
Clark, John 60,75,83,98,99
Clark, Jonathan 24,40
Clark, Mary 37
Clark, Rachel 138
Clark, Robert 60,74,75,93,97, 98,99,115,125,130,145
Clark, Thomas 7,33,60,74,75, 93,97,99,110,115,116
Clayton, Elizabeth 15
Clayton, George 15,102,103
Clements 87
Clements, Dr. 86,124,136
Clements, Ewen 135
Clements, Henry 136
Clements, Isaac 156
Clements, John 58,69,83,86,92, 97,107,108,114,122,156,157
Clements, Pitman (or Tilman) 128
Clerk, see Clark
Cloudas, Abner 115
Cloudas, John 60,98,99,115,130
Coale, William 65

Coats, Elizabeth 65
Coats, Samuel 9,40,64,106,107
Coats, Samuel Jr 107
Coats, Thomas 76,100
Coffland, see Coughland
Cole, Catherine 10
Cole, Elizabeth 9,40
Cole, Isaiah 106
Cole, John 107
Cole, Robert 82,106
Cole, Thomas 103,120
Cole, William 103
Coleman 87
Coleman, George 10,22,23,42, 43,57,67
Coleman, John 152
Coleman, Robert 4,35,53
Coleman, Robert Sp 25,66,72, 85,86,89,96,109
Coleman, Thomas 5,9,21,22,31, 39,46,47,53,68,69,85,87,91
Coleman, Whitehead 148
Coles, see Cole
Collens, William 120
Comp, see Kemp
Comp, John 87
Comton, see Compton
Compton 88
Compton, Richard 16,20,34,42
Cook, Samuel 82
Cook, Thomas 67
Cooper, Elizabeth 36,79,104, 121,139
Cooper, Elizabeth Jr 36
Cooper, Henry 101
Cooper, James 100
Cooper, Richard 16,103
Cooper, Thomas 10,37

Cooper, William 16,79
Corban, Corben, see Corbin
Corbin, Col. 100,117,131
Corbin, Mr. 11,38
Corbin, Richard 59,76
Cornelius, John 97,115,116
Cothron, see Cauthorn 134
Coughland, James 56,64,65,82
Covington 51,55,94,126,146
Covington, Luke 81,105,106, 107,123,140
Covington, Mr. 63
Covington, Richard 8,9,40,51, 65,82,106
Covington, William 1,3,5,6,9, 26,40,64,69,74,81,82,92,97, 105,106,107,151,156,157
Covington, William Jr 9
Covingtons Mill 3,29
Covingtons Mill Swamp 29,51, 55,63,71,94,111,126,146,150
Cox, Abner 104
Cox, Henry 24,41,65,84,85,112
Cox, John 11,16,36,37,71,82
Cox, Thomas 10,36,37,55,64, 71,79,94,103,104,121,122, 136,137,139
Cox, Thomas Jr 103,119
Cox, Thomas Sr 119
Cox, William 23,24,41,65,72, 84,85,95,108
Cox, William Jr 41,56
Crawford, Andrew 128
Creeks, see each one
  Gatewood, Glebe, Hoskins, Piscataway, Tylers
Cross, Joseph 90,91
Cross, Samuel 68,90,91

Croudas, see Crowdas
Crow, Isom   139
Crow, John   64,81,106,123,139
Crow, Susanna   105,123,139
Crow, William   9,39,55,81
Crowdas, John   34,75
Croxen, Croxson, see Croxton
Croxton, James   40,41
Croxton, John   4,18,23,25,30, 40,41,42,83,84,124,141
Croxton, Joseph   151
Croxton, Samuel   83,108,124
Croxton, Thomas   18,84,141
Cruden, Alexander   58,63,69,74, 76,92,125,144,156
Crutcher, Henry   12,32,33,61, 70,77,93,101,107,132
Crutcher, Henry Jr   77,101
Crutcher, Maberry   77
Crutcher, Richard   12
Crutcher, Thomas   82,106,107
Cumton, see Compton
Curtis, Christopher   6
Custis, James   4

Daley, Daniel   13,45,67
Daingerfield, William   5,6,13, 25,26,32,42,43,44,53,57,58, 66,69,74,92,156,157
Daingerfields Mill   86
Davis, Edward   17,43,67,89
Davis, Evan   75,120,137,138, 146,151
Davis, Humphrey   32,77
Davis, John   10,16,37,79,80,96, 103,104,120,122,138
Davis, Mary   90
Davis, Philip   137

Davis, Thomas   5,13,14,31,45, 73
Davis, William   6,7,138
Dayley, see Daley
Dea, Thomas   75
Dean, Benjamin   98
Dean, John   34
Dean, Thomas   6,28,34,54,60, 98,130
Degge, William   114
Degraffenried, Tscharner   94, 103
Dejarnett, James   149
Dennett, Thomas   80,94,105, 106,112,124,127,139,140, 146
Deshazo, John   64,82
Deshazo, William   64
Dick, Dicke, Dickes, Dike, see Dyke
Dickason, Dickenson, Dickinson, see Dickerson
Dickerson, John   81,105,123, 140
Dickerson, Thomas Cooper   91
Dickerson, Peter   29,40,51
Diggs, John   104
Discoll, Timothy   40
Dishazo, see Deshazo
Dix, James   3,9,10,65,81
Dix, Mary   16,17,42
Dix, Tandy   89
Dix, Thomas   89,128,148
Dix, William   16,17,42,43
Dobbins, Drury   105,111,124
Dobbins, Esther   140
Dobbins, Hester   105
Dobbins, Ruben   100
Dobbins, Thomas   100

Dobyns, Abner 61,77
Dobyns, Bowler 61
Dobyns, Daniel 2,8,10,12,37, 40,57,77
Dobyns, John 10,126,137
Dobyns, William 11,12,32
Dollerson, William 131
Dragon 1,2,3,28,29,32,49,50, 51,54,55,56,63,70,71,72,93, 94,95, 110,111,112,125, 126,127,145,146,147,149, 150,151
Driscoll, see Discoll
Duckworth, Rebeckah 6,7,33
Dudley, Samuel 156
Dun, see Dunn
Dunkin, Catherine 37
Dunn, Agrippa 123,124
Dunn, Benjamin 81,105,123, 139,140
Dunn, Elizabeth 139,140
Dunn, Henry 123
Dunn, James 132,133
Dunn, John 18,39,48,50,54,62, 70,78,93,101,102,118,119, 132,133
Dunn, Jonathan 64,72,106
Dunn, Nathaniel 124,141
Dunn, Philip 105
Dunn, Thomas 3,10,18,29,40, 49,51,55,64,70,71,80,81,82, 83,94,105,106,107,112,123, 124,138
Dunn, Wartuse 66
Dunn, William 3,18,19,26,30, 38,51,83,104,107,122,124, 138,139
Dunn, William (B) 141,147
Dunn, William (Black) 127
Dunn, William Jr 94,104,105, 123,124
Dunn, William Jr (B) 140
Dunn, William (W) 151
Dunn, William (White) 127,146
Dyke, John 2,14,28,38,50,54, 55,62,70
Dykes Mill 86

Eals, William 62
Edmondson, Constant 103, 119,136,137
Edmondson, Constantine 79
Edmondson, J 108,124
Edmondson, James 18,103, 108,119,125,137,141,144, 149,156
Edmondson, John 107,108, 112,124,141,149,156
Edmondson, John 18,19,30, 45,51,56,70,72,81,83,95
Edmondson, John Jr 102,128, 147
Edmondson, Philpar 79
Edmondson, Suckey 19,45
Edmondson, Thomas 10,26,30, 36,37,66,72,85
Edmondson, Thomas Jr 45
Edmondson, Tyler 79
Edmondson, William 11,57,67, 73,90,96,110,113,128,142, 151
Edmonson, see Edmondson
Edwards, John 38
Elliot 94
Elliots old field 3,29,51,55,71, 94,112,127,146,151

Evans 86
Evans, Charles 133
Evans, Dianna 133
Evans, Greensbe 48,62,101,
  111,118,119
Evans, John 2,5,8,10,26,32,49,
  61,62,77,78,101,102,118,
  132,133
Evans, John Jr 10,19,28,38,48,
  49,50,54,62,101,118
Evans, Joseph Jr 14
Evans, M 37
Evans, Micajah 29,37,51,55,
  64,102,111,118,119
Evans, Orphan 133
Evans, Thomas 13,45,133,145,
  150
Evans, Ursula 132,133
Evitt, Andrew 18

Falkner, see Faulkner
Fantilleroy, see Fauntleroy
Fargeson, see Ferguson
Ferguson, James 4,23
Ferguson, John 3,18,19,26,30,
  38,83,108,124
Ferguson, Titus 98,115,129,130
Faris, John 24
Farish, Mr. 18
Faulkner, David 20,34
Faulkner, Henry 14,62
Faulkner, Nicholas 86
Faulkner, Richard 102
Fauntleroy 128,129,148,152,
  153
Fauntleroy, John 73,90,114
Fauntleroy, William 22,35,90
Femester, James 39,76,82

Fergeson, Ferguson, see
  Farguson
Ferries, see each one
  Bowlers, Hardees, Little,
  Piscataway
Finney, James 3,9,29,51,56,71,
  94,112
Finnie, Finny, see Finney
Fisher, Benjamin 10,15,26,29,
  36,37,80,104
Fisher, James 15,29,36,37,130
Fisher, Orphans 80,104
Fisher, Richard 101,102
Fishers Mill 3
Fishers Mill Swamp 3,30,52,
  56,72,95,112,127,147,151
Fitsimmons, Gabriel 13
Fitsimmons, Garrett 45
Fitsimmons, Mary 90
Fitsjeffries, Betty 10
Fitsjeffries, Elizabeth 37
Fitsjeffries, Thomas 10
Fletcher, Orphans 6
Fletcher, William 6,37,79,103,
  112,119,123,137,138
Flitcher, see Fletcher
Fretwell, William 13,65,83,108
Fry, Capt. 38
Fry, Joshua 1,7,8,11,28,34
Fuller, Richard 132,134

Games, John 147
Games, Thomas 19,44,52,56,
  72,95,108,109,113,128
Gardner, Henry 118,126,132,
  133,150
Gardner, James 59
Garner, James 77
Garnett, Reuben 152

Gatewood 102
Gatewood Creek 126,145,150
Gatewood, Ambrose 73,89,96,
 109,113
Gatewood, Andrew 148
Gatewood, Augustine 143
Gatewood, Capt. 102
Gatewood, Caty 83,108
Gatewood, Cheney 128
Gatewood, Isaac 17,42,46,67,
 68,73,89,91,96
Gatewood, James 4,12,13,17,
 30,42,52,56,66,142
Gatewood, John 4,17,31,43,
 52,67,89
Gatewood, John Jr 17,42
Gatewood, John Sr 42
Gatewood, Joseph 152
Gatewood, Mary 143
Gatewood, Mr. 146
Gatewood, Patience 12
Gatewood, Philip 43,67,89,133
Gatewood, Richard 29,39,40,
 51,56,65,72,82,102,106,107,
 143
Gatewood, Thomas 16,20,34,
 88
Gatewood, William 3,12,18,19,
 21,26,46,57,66,67,68,69,91,
 126,133,134,136,143,150,
 152
Gatewood, William Jr 126,146
Gleab, Gleeb see Glebe
Glebe 11,38,100,117,131
Glebe Creek 1,28,49,54,70,93,
 110,125,145,149
Glebe land 59,76
Goar, John 6,8

Godfrey, Elizabeth 44
Godfrey, Peter 8,19
Good, John 122,138
Gorden, see Gordon
Gorden, Rod 43
Gordon, James 67,138,139
Gordon, Jane 17,42,43,89
Gordon, John 90,140
Gordon, Samuel 67
Gordon, Thomas 127,137,138,
 139,146
Gordon, Widow 67
Gordon, William 36,37,71,80,
 94,103,104,112,120,122,
 123
Graves, Thomas 23
Greenhill, James 43,45
Greenhill, Orphans 45
Greenhill, William 5,13,14,25,
 31,43,45,53,57,73,96,113,
 114,124
Greenwood, James 127
Greenwood, Richard 82,95,107
Greenwood, Rhodes 40,64,
 72,82,95,106,107,112
Greenwood, William 64,82,
 106,107,112,127
Greer, Robert 102
Gregg, John 66
Gresham, John 9
Grey, Charles 109
Griffing, James 89
Grissom, Samuel 138
Gude, see Good
Guill, Alexander 90

Hail, Hale, see Haile
Haile, Benjamin 34,42

Haile, John 16,17,34,52,57,66, 87,88
Haile, John Jr 20,26,34,73
Haile, Richard T. 152
Haile, Richard Thomas 113, 128,142,148
Haile, Thomas 42,110
Hailes Bridge 3,4,16,20,30,31, 51,52,56,57,72,73,95,96,112, 113,127,128,147,148,151, 152
Hale, see Haile
Hall, John Davis 10
Hames, William 37
Hammon, John 104
Hamor, William 10,11
Hardee, Andrew 7,8,14
Hardee, John 2,10,11,16,29,37
Hardee, Parrott 15
Hardee, Thomas 19
Hardees Ferry 4,19,30,52,56, 72,95,108,113
Hardy, see Hardee
Harper, Henry 20,22,52,57,66, 87
Harper, James 22,23
Harper, John 40,41,64,82,106, 107
Harpers Ordinary 3,29,51
Harrard (Harrerd), Thomas 41,65
Harrenton, James 41
Harwood, John 85
Harwood, Thomas 24
Hastie (Hasty), Thomas 12,32, 33
Hathaway, William 37
Haverton, see Howerton
Hayes, Henry 34

Hayes Ordinary 56
Hays, Edward 36,39
Hays, Isaac 103
Hays, John 2,28,104,122
Hays, William 138
Heard, Mr. 11
Herd, Mrs. 39
Hill 149
Hill, John 21,22,35,68,73,90, 91,96,114,143
Hill, Learn 54
Hill, Leonard 23,49,50,54,57, 58,68,69,70,73,75,78,91,93, 96,98,100,110,114,116,118, 125,130,145,149
Hill, Mr. 101,102
Hill, Orphans 49
Hill, Richard 90
Hill, Richard Jr 96,114
Hill, Thomas 64,76
Hilland, John 46
Hipkings, James 12
Hipkins 132
Hipkins, Andrew 61,62
Hipkins, Henry 153
Hipkins, Leroy 122,123
Hodges, Charles 38,39
Hodges, John 137
Hodges, Richard 40,41,65,83, 84
Hodgett, William 141
Hodghill, Daniel 23,83,124
Hold, see Holt
Holt 22
Holt, Richard 47,91
Holt, Richard Jr 127,141,147
Hoskins 25
Hoskins Bridge 128,147,152

Hoskins Creek 4,30,52,56,72, 88,95,113,142
Hoskins Swamp 21
Hoskins, John 10,37
Hoskins, Martha 10
Howard, Oliver 87
Howel, Orphans 47
Howell 22
Howerton, Heritage 106,107, 147,151
Howerton, James 39
Howerton, John 65,106,107
Howerton, Obediah 65,106, 107
Howerton, Thomas 9,39,40,64, 82,106,107
Howerton, William 106,147, 150,151
Howertons Ordinary 151
Hudson, Henry 12
Hudson, Vincent 61,62,77,99, 100,101
Hudsons Old Mill 118
Hull, Mary 42
Hull, William 17
Hundley, Robert 58,99,100, 116,117,125,130,131
Hundley, Thomas 99,100,116
Hunley, see Hundley
Hunt, John 16,17,42,43,52

Indian grant 41

James, Robert 10,103,121,136
Jeffries, John 62
Jeffries, Richard 62,63,78,102, 111,126,134,139,145,150

Johnson, Benjamin 4,19,26,31, 44,51
Johnson, Caty 136
Johnson, Elizabeth 62,77
Johnson, Griffin 100,132,134
Johnson, Henry 12,32,33
Johnson, Isaac 37
Johnson, James 100,101
Johnson, John 133
Johnson, Philip 38
Johnson, Richard 8,17,33,37, 61,103
Johnson, Robert 43,67,89
Johnson, Thomas 14,17,38,43, 62,77,78,134,145,150
Johnson, William 120
Jones, Ambrose 18,56,68,72, 83,95,108,109,113
Jones, Benjamin 23,65,108,109, 141,152
Jones, Erasmus 129,143,148, 153
Jones, Francis 13,18,22,31,53, 63,78,103,120,121
Jones, G 19
Jones, Gabriel 4,13,19,20,26, 30,44,45
Jones, Howel 45
Jones, James 4,19,30,45,52,55, 58,63,66,71,78,79,94,103, 111,126,134,135,136
Jones, John 7,83,98,107
Jones, Jonathan 18
Jones, Joseph 60
Jones, Orphans 130
Jones, Philip 15,18
Jones, Philip Dr 62

Jones, Richard 9,18,23,24,40,
  65,83,84
Jones, Richard Jr 83,84
Jones, Rebeckah 69,74,92,97
Jones, Rice 1,6,7,28,33,34,49,
  54,60,70,74,75,98,99,115,
  130
Jones, Robert 109
Jones, Thomas 7
Jones, William 38,39,45,60
Jordan, Isaac 120,122,127,138,
  139,150

Kemp 86,88
Kemp, Peter 20,34,109
Kid, see Kidd
Kidd, Henry 73,88,96,109,113,
  128,142,148,152
Kidd, Isaac 106,107,137
Kidd, James 111
Kidd, Philip 94,103,104,112,
  119,120,123,127,136,139,
  146,151
Kidd, Thomas 10,37
King & Queen County 3,4,5,
  16,29,31,51,52,53,56,57,58,
  72,90,95,96,112,113,114,
  127,128,147,148,151,152
Kircherval, John 147
Kirshevel, John 152
Knight, Maurice 19
Knight, Morris 45

Lacey, John 61
Landings 3,29,51,55,71,94,111,
  112
Langham, John 64
Langham, William 11,40
Latane 88

Latane, John 17,43,57,67,73,
  85,88,89,96,108,113,128
Latane, Lewis 156
Latane, Madame 24,25
Latane, Mary 41,42
Latane, William 148,152
Lay, John 33
Layford, Nicholas 35
Lee, Charles 33,60
Lee, Thomas 98
Lefon, Nicholas 23
Leverit 16
Leverit, Robert 10
Leverit, Robert Jr 11
Lewis, John 39
Little Ferry 4,30,52,56,72,95,
  113
Long Reach Road 3,4,30,52,56,
  72,95,112,127,147,151,152
Lourie, see Lowry
Lowry 26,63
Lowry, John 55,63,78,79,103
Lowry, Richard 89
Lowry, Thomas 78
Lowry, William 15,25,28,50,71,
  78,79,102
Lumpkin, John 24,41,84
Lunan, Patrick 77,78

Madearis, see Medearis
Maibell, John 137,138
Main Road 2,3,28,29,50,51,55,
  56,62,70,72,94,95,111,112,
  118,126,127,146,147,150,
  151
Man, see Mann
Mann, John 79,119,136,137
Mann, Joseph 39,64,82,103,
  107,119,120

Mann, Joseph Jr 82
Mann, Robert 103,120,136
Mann, Thomas 120
Marlow, Edward 9
Marlow, Mary 81,105,139,140
Marlow, Reuben 139
Marlow, William 105
Marsh, Robert 24
Marshall, Richard 12
Marshel, Hugh 136
Martin, Thomas 24
Mash, Robert 41
Mason, James 66
Mason, Thomas 81,105
Massey, John 6,7,33,60,74,75
Mathews Bridge 3,29,30,51,52,
  55,56,71,72,94,95,112,127,
  146,147,151
Matthews, William 9,16
May, John 89
Mays Ordinary 55
Mays, Edward 55
McCall, Alexander 135
McCall, Archibald 104,135
McCall, James 64,80
McCall, John 138
McCaul, see McCall
McDuff, Mr. 143
McIntosh, Lachlen 90
McTier, McTyor, see McTyre
McTyre, Josiah 75,97,110,115,
  116,129
Meador 86
Meador, John 142
Meador, Richard 142
Meador, Susanna 20,34
Meador, Thomas 20,86,142
Meador, William 20,34,88

Meadors Bridge 86
Medder, see Meador
Mearitt, John 35
Medearis, Charles 6,74,98
Medearis, John 33,75,97
Medley, James 11,28,38,39,50,
  59,117
Medley, James Jr 11,58,59,70,
  76,93,99,100,110,116,117,
  125,130,131
Medley, James Sr 11,76,99,100,
  117,131
Medley, John 11
Medley, John Sr 59
Mill Neck 5,25,31,43,53,57,73,
  96,113,148,152
Mill Swamp 2,28,50,55,63,70,
  71
Miller, Thomas 40,66,81,83,
  105,108,123,139
Mills, James 74,82,92,156
Mills, see each one
  Boughan, Boughton,
  Covington, Daingerfield,
  Dyke, Fisher, Hudson,
  Montague, Old, Smith,
  Waring, Waring Old, Webb
Minter, Francis 62
Minter, John 14,38,50,55,62,
  63,70,78,102
Minter, Joseph 115,130,138
Minter, Josiah 84,140,141
Miskell, Nenn 116
Mitchell, Edmond 102
Mitchell, Isaac 14,38,62,78
Mitchell, Jacob 78
Mitchell, John 118,119
Mitchell, Orphans 48,62

Mitchell, Peter 8
Mitchell, Sarah 101
Mitchell, Widow 134
Mitchell, William 14,33,38,62,
 78,111,134
Montague, Abraham 1,6,7,11,
 26,58,59,60,74,75,76,93,97,
 98,100,116,129,156
Montague, Capt. 33,34,60,115
Montague, Charlott 33,34
Montague, John 63,130
Montague, Lewis 60,74,97
Montague, Mrs. 38
Montague, Orphans 58, 59, 60
Montague, Samuel 74,98,115,
 116,130
Montague, William 6,7,33,47,
 60,75,92,97,98,99,101,102,
 114,115,118,119,125,129,
 130,133,144,156,158
Montagues Mill 98
Moody, George 17,42,43,52,
 67,89
Moody, Jeremiah 89
Moody, John 67
Moore, Augustine 148
Moore, Thomas 4,13
Mortimore, Dr. 143
Mullin, William 145
Munday, James 83,107

Neal, Ralph 100
Neale, Stephen 38,79
Newbill, George 9,29,40,51,64,
 72,82,95,106,107,112,118
Newbill, Henry 150
Newbill, James 9,29,40,64,82,
 106
Newbill, John 76

Newbill, Nathaniel 12,150
Newbill, Thomas 9,32,61,62,
 77,82,93,101,111,126,132,
 133,145
Newman, George 90

Old Mill 3,29,30,51,52,55,56,
 71,72,94,95,112,127,146,
 147,151
Old Mill Dam 118
Old Mill Swamp 93,94,111,
 113,126,145,150
Oneal, John 103,120,121
Oneale, James 79
Ordinary land 9
Ordinaries, see each one
 Harper, Hayes, Howerton,
 Mays, Webb
Oweing, John 149
Owen, Augustine 60,74,75,
 98,99,115
Owen, Elizabeth 15
Owen, John 101,130
Owen, William 115
Owens 135
Owens, Harwar 103
Owing, Haraway 153

Pace, John 6,7
Pace, Orphans 6,7
Padgett, Abraham 35
Padgett, Francis 23
Padgett, Henry 5,23
Padgett, John Jr 23
Padgett, Mary 18
Page, John 10,16,36
Page, Mann 19,42,44,108,109
Pagen, John 36
Pagett, Edmond 114

Pagget, John 35
Pain, Pane, see Paine
Paine, Orphans 7,47
Paine, John 36,75
Paine, Thomas 6,7,34,60
Pamplett, Nicholas 4
Pamplin, James 113
Pamplin, Nicholas 17,31,43, 67,89
Parker, Alexander 6,7,27,33, 53,156,157
Parker, Alexander Capt. 7,34, 43,44
Parker, Capt. 25,34
Parker, Mrs. 60,75
Parker, Susannah 74,75,98,99, 115
Parr, William 106
Parris, William 82
Parron, Tthomas 9
Parrott, James 34,38
Paterson, see Patterson
Patten, Grant 41
Patten, Robert 16
Patterson, John 59,99,101,134, 150
Patterson, Joseph 11,76,100
Patterson, Philip 61,77,100,116
Peachey, Capt. 15,16,36,47,80
Peachey, Mr. 62
Peachey, Samuel 48,49,93,101, 102,114,118,125,133,149, 157,158
Pead, Duell 156
Pearcey, Henry 15
Pendergrass, Edward 6
Pendleton, Nathaniel 14,15,21, 28,34,38,86

Pettes, Pette, see Pettis
Pettis 87,88
Pettis, John 20,34
Pettis, Orphans 87,88
Philips, see Phillips
Phillips, John 2,8,28,29,47,48, 49,50,54,55,71,94,111,118, 146,150
Phillips, Orphans 101
Phillips, Rev. 11,39
Phillips, Richard 126,133,145, 150
Phillips, William 1,5,26,31,32, 156
Phisimmons, see Fitsimmons
Pickett, John 13,19,24,41,65,84
Piles, Godfrey 14
Piles, Ludo (Ludy) 2,14,50,55, 63
Piles, Samuel 14,28,38,63,70, 78,102,134
Piscataway Creek 3,26,28,29, 30,51,55,71,78,93,94,111, 112,126,127,145,146,150, 151
Piscataway Ferry 1,2,4,19,27, 28,30,32,50,52,55,56,58,69, 70,72,74,92,94,97,108,110, 111,113,114,125,126,128, 137,144,146,147,149,150, 152
Piscataway Ferry Road 19
Piscataway Swamp 4,52,56,72, 88,95,112,127,147,152
Porter, William 113
Powell, John 24,41
Price, Ann 15
Price, Robert 17,24,41,43,67

Profnall, James 14
Prossor, William 138
Purkins, Cary 18
Purkins, Geoffrey 40
Purkins, Griffin 40
Purkins, Henry 18,66,79,83, 108,124,141
Purkins, J 153,158
Purkins, Lucy 65,82
Purkins, William 141

Quarters 1,2,11,14,15,28,34,38, 49,50,51,54,55,65,6670,71, 78,93,94,110,111,125,126, 145,146,149,150

Radford, George 18
Radford, Jonathan 83
Ramsey, Orphan 137
Ramsey, William 83,104,105, 122,123,137,138
Ray, John 89
Reaves, see Reeves
Reeves, Ann 13
Reeves, George 20,34,88
Reeves, Henry 12,20,25,43,44, 86
Reeves, James 31,44,57,73,89, 96
Reeves, Joseph 4,24,25,31,41, 52,65,84,85,108
Reeves, Joseph Jr 31,44
Reeves, Orphans 86,87
Rennolds, Elizabeth 143
Rennolds, James 5,21,22,27,31, 46,53,57,73,96,114,157
Rennolds, John 21,22,57,124, 143,148,153
Rennolds, John Jr 143

Rennolds, Robert 21,22
Rennolds, Sarah 68,91,143
Rennolds, Sthreshlye 143
Rennolds, William 21,22,46,68, 91
Rennoles, Reynolds, see Rennolds
Richards, John 103,111,125, 134,135,157
Richeson, James 60,75
Richeson, Peter 60
Richeson, William 7,33
Ridgaway, Anthony 33
Right, see Wright
Ritchie, Alexander 125
Ritchie, Archibald 114,144,157
Roan, see Roane
Roane 129,148
Roane, Alexander 47
Roane, Col. 153
Roane, Maj. 88
Roane, Thomas 43,67,76,83, 89,100,108,114,124,125, 141,144,157
Roane, W 49
Roane, William 1,17,27,42,43, 58,69,89,92,125,129,141, 143,144,148,149,157,158
Roberts, Jane 10
Roberts, Orphans 17
Robinson 38
Robinson, Col. 2,14.26,28,29, 50,55,70,71,78,94,102,111
Robinson, Henry 26
Robinson, John 1,5,15,25,39, 48,63,157
Rodden, John 10,16,37,79,103, 119,120,137,138
Roden, see Rodden

Ross, John 39
Ruller, Richard 126,134
Russell 133
Russell, George 38,48,101,102, 118,119
Russell, Joseph 56
Rust[?], Benjamin 63
Ryland, Joseph 65,84,85,127, 141
Ryland, Thomas 147

Sacry, Simon 10
Sadlar, John 115,116,129
Sale, Leonard 68
Salt, Thomas 7,60
Sanders, see Saunders
Saunders, Abraham 125,145
Saunders, Alexander 99,101, 125,131
Saunders, Alexander S 117
Saunders, Ann 59
Saunders, Charles 38,76,117, 131,145,149
Saunders, George 133
Saunders, John 76
Saunders, Joseph 54,58,59,76
Saunders, Orphans 76,117
Scandret, Scandreth, see Scandrett
Scandrett, Isaac 1,4,13,25,27, 43,44,53,57,69,73,74,89,157
Scott, David 4,20
Sears, Seares, see Seayres
Seayres, John 5,13,31,23,36,45, 53
Seayres, Robert 22,23,35
Segar, John 74
Shackelford, Richard 82

Shackleford, Maj. 117,131
Shackleford, Roger 107
Shaw, Samuel 20
Shearwood, Jacob 83,108,124, 141
Shearwood, Jonathan 113
Shelton, see Skelton
Shelton, Crispin 15,16
Shelton, James 33
Shelton, Mary 33
Shelton, Ralph 7
Shelton, Reuben 74,75,97,115, 116
Shelton, Thomas 7
Shepard, Shephard, see Shepherd
Shepherd, Ephraim 82,106
Shepherd, Elizabeth 40
Shepherd, Jeremiah 8,9,40,61, 65
Shepherd, Jeremiah Jr 9,12,32
Shepherd, Jeremy 3,12
Shepherd, Orphans 77
Shepherd, William 100,145,150
Sheridan, Isaac 137
Sheridan, John 36,80,104
Sheridan, Orphans 80
Sherwood, see Shearwood
Ship, Gideon 152
Shorthose, Henry 156
Shurdan, see Sheridan
Sillivan, see Sullivan
Simcoe, Thomas 82,107
Simcox, see Simcoe
Simes, Thomas 12
Singleton, John 66
Skelton, James 18
Skelton, Mr. 18

Smether, John 46,68,91
Smether, William 68,69
Smith 129,148,153
Smith, Abraham 128
Smith, Alexander 142,152
Smith, Ann 38
Smith, Augustine 25,113
Smith, Benjamin 36,51,55,71,
  94,104,112
Smith, Capt. 26,104,132,148
Smith, Col. 3,29,51
Smith, Francis 12,22,25,26,27,
  31,32,33,35,39,49,61,63,69,
  74,77,90,92,97, 100,102,103,
  132,133,157
Smith, Gregory 17,43
Smith, James 99
Smith, John 8,18,23,33,38,41,
  48,54,59,61,62,70,76,83,93
  108,116,117,124,128,130,
  143
Smith, Laurence 131
Smith, Meriwether 77,102,125,
  135,136,144,157
Smith, Nicholas 2,6,12,16,27,
  32,33,61,69,77,92,93,101,
  157
Smith, Nicholas Jr 12,28,50,
  54,61,62,70,77
Smith, Orphans 47,116,130
Smith, Samuel 32,33,50,54,62,
  77,88,117,130,131
Smith, Thomas 7,152
Smith, Widow 11,99
Smith, William 19,44,45,72,85,
  87,132,135,136,144,148,158
Smiths Mill 10,132
Snodgrass, William 122
Soan 26

Souls, John 19
Southern, William 131
St. John, Abraham 16,61
St. John, Isaac 18
St. John, James 13,84
St. John, John 12,32
St. John, Mary 39
St. John, Richard 106,107,147,
  151
St. John, Thomas 4,13,30
St. John, William 3,9
Staines, Elizabeth 82
Staint, Elizabeth 40
Sthreshely, Thomas 35
Sthreshley, Hannah 21,23
Sthreshley, Thomas 23,129,
  143,148,153
Sthreshley, William 21,22
Stockley, Diana 6,7,33,34
Stone, John 44
Street, Henry 97,115,116,129,
  145
Street, Richard 97,110,115,116,
  125,129,145,149
Stuart, Henry 65
Stuart, William 53,156,157
Sullivan, Daniel 22,23,35,46,68
Sullivan, Daniel Jr 68
Sullivan, James 91
Sullivant, see Sullivan
Surveyor 25,26
Swelivan, Swillivan, see Sullivan
Swilby, John 57

Taff, Thomas 60,74,98,99,115,
  130
Tandy 129,148,153
Tandy, Henry 5,22,23,31,36,53,
  57,73,96,114,124

Tandy, Silvanus 57,96
Tate, Arthur 106,107,123
Tate, Mr. 104
Tayloe, Col. 3,29,71,94,111
Tayloe, John Col. 15
Taylor 86
Taylor, Berry 80,105,122
Taylor, Francis 33
Taylor, George 80
Taylor, James 87
Taylor, John 138
Taylor, Orphan 138
Thacker, Edwin 86
Thomas, Matthew 67
Thomson, Samuel 24
Thomson, Thomas 7
Townley, John 56,64,65,82,107
Towns, Mr. 39
Trebble, Treble, see Trible
Tribble, Tribles, see Trible
Trible, John 10,37
Trible, Orphans 120,121
Trible, Peter 19,120,136
Trible, Robert 103
Trible, William 10,37
Tureman, William 82,106
Turner, Elkanah 138
Turner, George 9,16,36,80
Turner, James 3,9,16,26,36,80,
    104,122,123
Turner, Thomas 122,138
Tyler, Capt. 28,50,54
Tyler, Col. 51,55
Tyler, John 3,15,18,36,63,64,
    80,83,123
Tyler, Orphans 123
Tyler, Richard 28,39,50,55,63,
    71,79,93

Tyler, William 15,26,36
Tylers Creek 2,28,50,54,70,111

Upper precinct 5,13,21,31,46,
    53,58,68,73,90,96,114
Upshaw, Forrest 21,22,46,53,
    57,67,68,73,89
Upshaw, Hannah 21,22,46,68
Upshaw, Hannah Jr 91
Upshaw, James 67,73,90,96
Upshaw, Jeremiah 43
Upshaw, Jeremy 17
Upshaw, John 22,58,68,69,74,
    91,92,97,110,114,125,143,
    144,149,157,158
Upshaw, Richard 5,21,22,31,
    35,46,47,53,68
Upshaw, William Jr 68

Vass, Henry 69,74,76,77,91,92,
    114,117,129,131,143,144,
    158
Vass, John 1,5,6,11,26,27,31,
    32,49,53,58,69,77,79,103,
    121,136,157,158
Vass, John Jr 51,55,64,121
Vass, John Sr 59
Vass, Mr. 38,39
Vass, Reuben 59
Vass, Vincent 59,76,96

Waganer, all spellings, see
    Waggener
Waggener, Benjamin 5,13,14,
    31,45,46,53,90,109,114,124,
    142,148,152
Waggener, Elizabeth 86,88
Waggener, Herbert 20,34

Waggener, James 13
Waggener, Nathan 124,129, 142,143,148
Waggener, Reuben 88,113
Waggener, Samuel 20,34
Wale, Thomas 110
Walker, Charles 31
Waller, Charles 53,57,73,96,114
Waller, William 21,22,46
Wareing, see Waring
Waring 96
Waring, Col. 114,124
Waring, Francis 69,91,124
Waring, R P 142,143
Waring, Robert P 148
Waring, Robert Payne 124,128
Waring, Robert Sd 142
Waring, Thomas 58,69,90,92, 109,157
Waring, Thomas Jr 13,31,35, 36,45,46,53,57
Warings Mill 4,5,20,30,31,52, 53,57,73,96,114,128,148
Warings Mill Swamp 4,16,30, 31,52,57,73,96,128,148,152
Warings Old Mill 20,96,113, 124,129,148,153
Warings Old Mill Swamp 142, 148
Watkins, John 5,22,31,46,47
Watkins, Lewis 39,64
Watkins, Orphans 131
Watkins, William 68,69,73,91, 96,103,107,114
Wattkins, see Watkins
Watts, Mary 130,138
Watts, Thomas 100,115,117, 131
Watts, William 117
127,146
Webb, Capt. 101,102
Webb, Edward 23,35
Webb, James 103,105,110,111, 112,114,120,122,123,124, 125,127,130,131
Webb, James 2,9,12,15,27,32, 50,58,69,71,74,78,79,80,81, 82,92,93,94,97,134,135,137, 144,145,146,150,157,158
Webb, James Jr 103
Webb, John 2,8,15,28,48,49,62, 63,70,78,80,118,133,140, 151
Webb, John Jr 102,127,146
Webb, Mary 138
Webb, Mr. 71,104
Webb, Old 7
Webb, Thomas 140
Webb, William 114,129,140, 148,153
Webbs Mill 126,146,150
Webbs Ordinary 71,94,112,127
Wellman, Matthew 13
Wells, Absalom 22,47
Wells, James 126
White, John 33
White, Robert 124
Whites Run Bridge 4,30,52,56, 72,113,128,147,152
Wiley, John 54,60,70,75
Williams, Ann 15
Williams, Hugh 2,7,8,28,33
Williams, Isaac 62,101,118,133
Williams, John 137
Williams, Reuben 62
Williams, Richard 14
Williams, Thomas 8,47
Williams, Williamson 140

Williams, William 137
Williamson, Edward 37
Williamson, Else 138
Williamson, Isaac 122,138
Williamson, John 15,16,36,79,
 80,82,104,105,121,122,123,
 124,138,140
Williamson, John Jr 16,36,120
Williamson, Leonard 36,80,104
Williamson, Richard 122,138
Williamson, Robert 82
Williamson, Thomas 3,10,15,
 16,36,37,51,55,64,71,80,94,
 103,104,111,119,120,126,
 139,150
Williamson, Thomas Jr 10
Williamson, William 10,37,79,
 121
Williamson, William Jr 16
Willson, see Wilson
Wilson, Charles 10
Wilson, Hugh 21,86,87,141
Wilson, Joseph 35
Wodleton, see Woodlington
Wood, Thomas 140,141,142,
 147,151
Wood, William 74
Woodlington, Thomas 23,24
Woolbanks, William 23
Wright, Ambrose 72,83,84,85,
 95,108,112
Wright, Elizabeth 126,127,138,
 146
Wright, George 4,24,25,30,41,
 42,52,65,84,85
Wright, George Jr 41
Wright, James 84
Wright, Mrs. 150,151

Wrights Landing 127,146
Wyatt, Thomas 56,66

Yarington, William 11
Yarrington, John 149
Young 26
Young, Godfrey 100
Young, Henry 2,14,15,26,27,
 32,39,48,63,78,79,126,133,
 134,135,145,150,157
Young, John 2,8,14,15,26,28,
 39,48,49,50,54,70,93,102,
 111,118
Young, Mary 77,109,119,126,
 132,146,150
Young, Mrs. 102
Young, Orphans 63,78
Young, Smith 102,103,111,135,
 136
Young, William 90,92,97,99,
 102,103,110,114,125,132,
 134,135,144,146,149,150,
 157,158
Young, William Jr 132,133,
 146,150
Young, Williamson 15,28,33,
 39,48,78,79,102
Younger, James 40
Younger, Thomas 18,23,24

www.ingramcontent.com/pod-product-compliance
Lightning Source LLC
Chambersburg PA
CBHW050800160426
43192CB00010B/1585